THE LAYMAN'S BIBLE COMMENTARY

THE LAYMAN'S BIBLE COMMENTARY
IN TWENTY-FIVE VOLUMES

THE LAYMAN'S
BIBLE COMMENTARY

Balmer H. Kelly, *Editor*

Donald G. Miller *Associate Editors* **Arnold B. Rhodes**

Dwight M. Chalmers, *Editor,* **John Knox Press**

VOLUME 11

THE BOOK OF
ISAIAH

G. Ernest Wright

JOHN KNOX PRESS

ATLANTA

© M. E. Bratcher 1964

10   9   8   7   6   5   4   3

Complete set: ISBN: 0-8042-3086-2
This volume: 0-8042-3071-4
Library of Congress Card Number: 59-10454
First paperback edition 1982
Printed in the United States of America
John Knox Press
Atlanta, Georgia 30365

PREFACE

The LAYMAN'S BIBLE COMMENTARY is based on the conviction that the Bible has the Word of good news for the whole world. The Bible is not the property of a special group. It is not even the property and concern of the Church alone. It is given to the Church for its own life but also to bring God's offer of life to all mankind—wherever there are ears to hear and hearts to respond.

It is this point of view which binds the separate parts of the LAYMAN'S BIBLE COMMENTARY into a unity. There are many volumes and many writers, coming from varied backgrounds, as is the case with the Bible itself. But also as with the Bible there is a unity of purpose and of faith. The purpose is to clarify the situations and language of the Bible that it may be more and more fully understood. The faith is that in the Bible there is essentially one Word, one message of salvation, one gospel.

The LAYMAN'S BIBLE COMMENTARY is designed to be a concise, non-technical guide for the layman in personal study of his own Bible. Therefore, no biblical text is printed along with the comment upon it. This commentary will have done its work precisely to the degree in which it moves its readers to take up the Bible for themselves.

The writers have used the Revised Standard Version of the Bible as their basic text. Occasionally they have differed from this translation. Where this is the case they have given their reasons. In the main, no attempt has been made either to justify the wording of the Revised Standard Version or to compare it with other translations.

The objective in this commentary is to provide the most helpful explanation of fundamental matters in simple, up-to-date terms. Exhaustive treatment of subjects has not been undertaken.

In our age knowledge of the Bible is perilously low. At the same time there are signs that many people are longing for help in getting such knowledge. Knowledge of and about the Bible is, of course, not enough. The grace of God and the work of the Holy Spirit are essential to the renewal of life through the Scriptures. It is in the happy confidence that the great hunger for the Word is a sign of God's grace already operating within men, and that the Spirit works most wonderfully where the Word is familiarly known, that this commentary has been written and published.

THE EDITORS AND
THE PUBLISHERS

THE BOOK OF

ISAIAH

INTRODUCTION
ISAIAH 1-39

In the Book of Isaiah, Israel's prophetic literature reaches its
zenith in both religious profundity and artistic expression. Indeed,
especially within the second part of the book, poetic intensity
frequently becomes lyrical, possessing a singular beauty matched
only by certain of the Psalms. Here the prophetic faith in God
has exercised such a purifying effect that the forms of expression
have become remarkable vehicles for conveying the prophetic
message.

From the earliest times, however, people have pondered the
words and wondered about their meaning. The evangelist Philip
encountered a high official of the Ethiopian government who was
reading a scroll of this book as he was riding in his chariot on
his way home from Jerusalem. Philip said, "Do you understand
what you are reading?" The man replied, "How can I, unless
someone guides me?" (Acts 8:30-31). The writing is so much a
part of its time and culture that it requires study and interpretation. Not only the question, "What does it say?" but also the
more insistent query, "What does it mean?" have been the occasion for centuries of study and commentary.

The Isaiah Literature

During the course of the last one hundred years the Church's
most productive scholarship has come to the almost unanimous
conclusion that we must think of the Book of Isaiah as the literature of a particular prophetic school. This Isaiah school of disciples preserved and brought together into one large scroll material centering in the words of two great personalities. One of
these lived during the second half of the eighth century B.C., at a
time of great crisis when the Assyrian army made repeated invasions of Palestine in preparation for the conquest of Egypt.

The other lived two centuries later, during the second half of the sixth century, when Jerusalem was in ruins, when the Persians were taking over the whole of the Near East, and when the ancient world was full of excitement at the dawn of a new day. These two prophets are called "First Isaiah" and "Second Isaiah," and the division of the material which marks the beginning of the words of the latter is at chapter 40.

How can we be certain of such a view? The first verse of the Book of Isaiah appears to say that the book is "the vision of Isaiah the son of Amoz," and the date is given according to the reigns of Judean kings in the eighth century. Is that not a fact sufficient to settle the question of authorship? Yet all agree that when we study chapters 40-66 we find ourselves in the Persian period, two centuries later than the time of Isaiah the son of Amoz. In the past, those who have defended the single authorship of the book believed that Isaiah simply uttered true prophecies about things in the future. It must be said that this is a possibility; the predictive element is indeed an integral part of prophecy. Yet the prophet, as we shall see, understood that God had appointed him to an office in the divine government of the world. In that office it was his duty to report to Israel and to the world certain governmental decrees and decisions which the divine Sovereign wished his people to know.

While surrounding peoples made use of divination, spiritualism, and a variety of magical practices in the attempt to determine the will of the gods, such superstition was forbidden Israel. Instead, Israel is informed, God will raise up one of their own brethren as a prophet and will put words in his mouth that he may speak as commanded (Deut. 18:9-22). The world of the occult is forbidden. What God wants Israel to know, he will reveal by means of his spokesman. The prophet thus had messages for his own people in his own day. It would not be within the primary function of his office to address another people in another time than his own. For this reason students of prophecy have suggested the following as a rule of thumb: *a prophecy is earlier than what it predicts, but contemporary with, or later than, what it presupposes.* In "First Isaiah" the prophet *predicts* the destruction of his people by the Assyrian army and *presupposes* the political situation of the eighth century. In chapters 40-55, on the other hand, the prophet *predicts* the return of Israel to Palestine by the power of God working through the Persian emperor Cyrus, who will bring the Babylonian empire to an end. He *presupposes* that Israel is in exile, that Jerusalem is in ruins, and that the most important man on the horizon at the moment is Cyrus. This means that God's spokesman is sent with a message to a scattered and depressed people after the destruction of Judah and Jerusalem by the Babylonian emperor Nebuchadnezzar in 587 B.C., but just before Cyrus the Persian takes Babylon and releases subject peoples in 539-538 B.C.

Chapters 56-66 *predict* a "new heavens" and a "new earth," but *presuppose* that some Judeans have returned to Jerusalem and have rebuilt or are rebuilding the Temple. At least this would appear to be the implication of such verses as: "My house [temple] shall be called a house of prayer for all peoples" (56:7) and "Heaven is my throne and the earth is my footstool; what is the house [temple] which you would build for me . . .?" (66:1). Consequently, while some interpreters used to speak of a "Third Isaiah" for these chapters, it is today more commonly supposed that they come from Second Isaiah and his disciples in the period between 538 and 500 B.C.

How were the words of the prophets preserved? This is a question for which we have far too little information. We can be sure, however, that the prophets themselves did not write them. Only a comparatively few people bothered to write in those days. Writing was a special trade, the profession of the scribe, who was comparable perhaps to the stenographer of our time. On one very special occasion when Jeremiah was forbidden to speak in public, he dictated a summary of all his prophecies to his companion, Baruch (Jer. 36); but that is thought to have been an unusual incident and not a typical occurrence. The biblical day was a time when memory was highly developed and culture was something transmitted orally from generation to generation. People did not depend upon books for knowledge. They depended upon memory and teachers.

The prophetic messages were given in the form of a highly sophisticated and exalted poetry. Why this was the case, we do not know. Yet the inspiration of Israel's great prophets was of a type that elevated both intellectual and artistic expression to such a high point that we must say that Hebrew prophecy is a phenomenon unparalleled in the world's history. How the prophetic poetry was produced is a mystery. Was it a carefully prepared series of compositions by the prophet? Like the great poem on

love in I Corinthians 13, a few passages composed or quoted
appear to be of this nature. Yet for the most part we must think
of highly gifted men, disciplined by a commitment which was so
absolute as to permit no interference from the outside. Their concentration on God and their ecstatic inspiration were so intense
as to unite their whole being in one elevated expression of the
will of God. Theirs was a great tradition of faith, and their knowledge of it and their singlehearted concentration upon faith's Object led them to vocal expression far beyond anything normally
expected as possible.

If such is the case, then we cannot think in terms of literary
compositions carefully written and preserved. We must instead
think of oral composition which was given under the intensity of
inspiration, portions of which were remembered by the prophet
himself and by his disciples. It was the prophetic disciples who
took upon themselves the transmission and preservation of the
words of their master. They do not give us verbatim reports of
entire prophetic messages but only portions which were remembered. Sometimes the original poetry has been lost and summaries
are preserved mainly in prose, as is the case, for example, in
chapters 7-8 of Isaiah. In the course of time certain anonymous
prophetic words from the "School of Isaiah" came to be included
with the materials of the master. In the Book of Isaiah samples
of such prophecy appear in chapters 13-14 and 24-27, among
others.

The Identity of the Prophet

The story of the prophet Micaiah in I Kings 22 may be taken
as depicting the setting of the prophetic message between the
ninth and sixth centuries B.C. The Aramean kingdom of Damascus about 850 B.C. holds Israelite territory across the Jordan.
King Ahab of Israel has called the Judean king, Jehoshaphat, to
his aid because they have a mutual assistance pact. But before
the armies set forth for battle the will of the Lord is desired. A
pagan army would have used a diviner. David a century before
might have used Urim and Thummim, the sacred dice carried by
the chief priest. But at least since the time of Samuel one central
tradition was that God had instituted the office of prophet as a
means whereby he could speak freely to the king about what he
should do.

Ahab, in any event, is surrounded by prophets, all of whom tell him piously that he is to go to battle because God is going to make him victorious. Jehoshaphat, from a more conservative environment in Jerusalem, appears unconvinced by this prophetic babbling. He asks whether there is not someone else from whom enquiry can be made. Ahab answers that there is one prophet, the man Micaiah, but says, "I hate him, for he never prophesies good concerning me, but evil." Nevertheless Micaiah is called, though he is solemnly warned in advance that if he knows what is good for him he will speak as the other prophets have done. After mimicking the words of the popular prophets, Micaiah finally says: "Hear the word of the LORD: I saw the LORD sitting on his throne, and all the host of heaven standing beside him on his right hand and on his left; and the LORD said, 'Who will entice Ahab, that he may go up and fall at Ramoth-gilead?' And one said one thing, and another said another. Then a spirit came forward and stood before the LORD, saying, 'I will entice him. . . . I will . . . be a lying spirit in the mouth of all his prophets.'" Micaiah also says: "I saw all Israel scattered upon the mountains, as sheep that have no shepherd."

Behind the great prophets there was this symbolic vision: A heavenly courtroom, presided over by the universal Ruler—a trial scene in which Israel is found guilty and where sentence is decreed to be carried out by a historical enemy of Israel. The prophet understands himself to be the official of that heavenly court, charged with making the decree public among those who have been sentenced. There is always a possibility that those who hear may repent so that God may stay the sentence. In this sense the prophet can be understood also as a watchman, charged by God with warning the people of their dire peril (see Jer. 6:17; Ezek. 3:17), or as an "assayer and tester," that the people be refined (Jer. 6:27-30).

While Micaiah's announcement is a word against King Ahab, he stands at a moment when a great change in emphasis is beginning to be made among a group of conservatives in the Northern Kingdom. This is to the effect that Israel has so broken her pact, her treaty or Covenant with God, that God is about to declare the whole relationship abrogated and deliver Israel to the destroyers. As this theme is taken up by the eighth and seventh century prophets, they encounter a people who will have none of it, but who by cult and political maneuvering attempt to achieve

security without any assumption of responsibility for treaty violation, without faith or confession. And as the prophets testify, all
such cheap maneuvers fail. This, then, is the background of the
prophecies of judgment.

The prophet Amos, who preceded Isaiah by a few years, and
the prophet Hosea, who was his contemporary in the Northern
Kingdom in his early years, were messengers of God's judgment.
Israel had been brought to trial in God's heavenly court and had
been found guilty of flagrant breach of Covenant. The sentence
was destruction at the hands of Assyria and a new exile from the
land.

Consider this time in which these prophets lived. It was the
era of history's first great imperialistic wars, the poles of power
being on the Euphrates and the Nile. But the great days of Egypt
were over. And now Assyria, and then Babylonia, found Palestine
a troublesome problem on the border of Sinai en route to Egypt.
Hence they insisted on peace and stability in that country, and
when it was not forthcoming, after warning, they simply laid both
Northern and Southern Kingdoms waste, destroyed every sizable
town, killed most of the inhabitants, and carried the leaders off
into exile and transplantation.

This was the era of the prophets, and these were the events
they were talking about.

People frequently say: What is the good of learning about the
Bible as a series of past events? How does it all become contemporary? What good does it do to learn about the God of history and the mighty acts whereby he was confessed? How is he
contemporary, in the here and now? The best answer is that of
John Calvin: The Scriptures become the spectacles which enable
us to see and bring things into focus now, but without which all
would be confused. And, further, it has been the Church's experience that in the study of the Scriptures, God by his Spirit
brings them alive, if we read expectantly and at the same time
face our own situation as resolutely as the prophets faced theirs.

One might well have said in the prophets' time: What good is
it to talk about the mighty acts of God in forming the nation
centuries ago? Does this mean, as the popular prophets are saying, that all is going to be well with us, that God has only one
attribute, namely love, and that he therefore will not do anything
but love and help us? The prophets were those who read the
signs of the times and made the classical confession contempo-

rary. They knew the nature of God, his independence, and the conditions of the Covenant with Israel. They knew the long history of their nation well, and in particular its massive failure to achieve and maintain a political and economic order that in any way reflected the will of God. Threatened with being swallowed up also by the great imperialistic armies of the time, they simply put matters together in terms of the righteousness of God. The whole historical situation meant only one thing: in the complete flouting of every consideration of loyalty and justice, while attempting to buy off the demands of God with elaborate worship, Israel was doomed.

Yet the righteousness of God was also known to be redemptive. Hence the prophets could pray for repentance, and they could also proclaim a future beyond the impending destruction. Indeed, the present or coming terror is but the first step which God is taking toward the creation of the new age, when the desperate problems of the present will be resolved in the New Covenant, the new humanity, the new earth. But we note here the anticipation of what is to be central in the New Testament: Given life in this world as it is in rebellion against its Lord, there is no use in hoping for peace apart from judgment. Where there is gross evil, there will be no peace—only blood, fear, terror, suffering. Sin and death cannot be separated. And the only road to life is through the suffering. We, of course, want a future without anxiety and without blood, and we are very clever at devising schemes to get it, to circumvent the suffering. But, says the prophet—as also does the Cross of the New Testament—the door to hope is only through the valley of the shadow; the glory of God will become apparent only to those who have faced the darkness. Hence, in neither of the Testaments is religious faith or practice a guide to successful and happy life. It is rather a sure anchor in a heaving sea. It is a struggle to discover one's vocation and the vocation of God's people in a sinful and alien world, to praise the Lord for his marvelous goodness, committing one's way entirely to him but without any certainty that history is organized for one's personal security.

Perhaps enough has been said to suggest the importance of the biblical conception of historical reality, of the extreme sensitivity which the theology gave to the apprehension of evil, injustice, and dishonor in the world; and withal the joy and confidence of a faith cast adrift, as it were, within history but never doubting the everlasting arms below. Here is the basis for much Christian concern today about the "popular" church, accommodating Christians for whom faith is a device to ensure success, little more than a built-in optimism that confirms the self-righteous, an opiate which attempts to render the whole Christian enterprise in earth as little more than pretty and petty.

The Early Years of First Isaiah

The prophetic ministry of Isaiah took place in Jerusalem in the half-century between about 740 and 690 B.C. One usually begins the study of the book with the prophet's autobiographical story in chapter 6 of his call to prophesy. There he says that the call came "in the year that King Uzziah died" (6:1). Unfortunately, that year cannot be fixed with certainty.

During the third quarter of the eighth century both the kingdom of Israel in the north and the kingdom of Judah in the south had enjoyed great prosperity under two very able kings, Jeroboam I and Uzziah respectively. Toward the end of that period, about 760-750 B.C., the Judean Amos had prophesied in Israel that the great era of peace was soon to end and that God was about to destroy the nation and send the people who survived into exile (Amos 2:13-16; 5:2, 27; 6:14). For this he was accused of treason against Jeroboam by the high priest of the royal temple at Bethel and told to go back to Judah, whence he had come (7:10-13).

About 748 B.C., Jeroboam II died, and his death plunged the Northern Kingdom into an unstable political situation which lasted until the destruction which Amos had prophesied came about in 724-21 B.C. Menahem (about 748-738 B.C.) was the only king who managed to hold his position for as long as ten years, and he was helped in this by becoming a vassal of the Assyrian emperor, Tiglath-pileser III (Pul), and paying him a very heavy tribute (II Kings 15:17-20). Tiglath-pileser (745-728 B.C.) in one of his inscriptions confirms the biblical account of this. The Assyrian says of Menahem, "I returned him to his place [and imposed tribute upon him,] gold, silver, linen garments with multicolored trimmings . . ." In a series of ostraca found in the excavations of Samaria, Israel's capital, we have records of wine and olive oil shipments from wealthy landowners, which may indeed represent the special tribute which Menahem is said to have exacted from the wealthy in Israel according to II Kings 15:20.

It was during the reign of Tiglath-pileser that Assyrian pressure on the west became so strong that it could not be withstood. Of particular interest is the fact that the monarch tells us in his own inscriptions that during his early campaigns against Syria he was confronted with a large western coalition of forces headed by King Uzziah of Judah. This cannot mean that Uzziah himself was the general at the head of the combined forces. The Bible tells us that "he was a leper to the day of his death, and he dwelt in a separate house. And Jotham the king's son was over the household [prime minister], governing the people of the land" (II Kings 15:5). Nevertheless, Uzziah's leprosy seems not to have prevented him from exercising an able and vigorous rule. Judging from the inscriptions of Tiglath-pileser, Uzziah must have been one of the strongest political forces of the west, with the most stable government. Otherwise he would not have been the political head of the western coalition.

Since Uzziah (or Azariah) was still king during the two-year reign of Menahem's son and successor and also at the start of the reign of the army general, Pekah, who slew that son and reigned in his stead (II Kings 15:23-27), it seems likely that Uzziah's long reign may have extended from about 769 to 734 B.C. In any case, during the last sixteen years of his life his son Jotham had shared the rule with his father and did not long survive him.

As was the case with all the great prophets about whom we have information, Isaiah's call from the Lord came at a most critical juncture. The great king and leader of the west against Assyria was dead. New pressure from Tiglath-pileser was beginning; and the new king on the throne in Jerusalem was Ahaz, Jotham's son. Our meager information about his reign seems to indicate that he was a man of weak and unstable character. One of his first political acts was to withdraw Jerusalem and Judah completely from the coalition. This was the occasion of the Syro-Ephraimite war. Pekah, king of Israel, and Rezin, king of the Aramean ("Syrian") state centered in Damascus, immediately declared war on Ahaz to force Judah to remain in the coalition (II Kings 16:5). At this time the famous meeting of Isaiah with Ahaz, as described in Isaiah 7, took place. We are there told that the king and his people were so frightened by the threat that "his heart and the heart of his people shook as the trees of the forest shake before the wind" (7:2). We are further informed that the plan of coalition was to remove Ahaz from the throne and to put in his place "the son of Tabe-el" (7:6). This name is known from an Assyrian inscription as an Aramean land, probably in northern Transjordan. The identity of "the son of Tabe-el" is thus completely unknown, except that he was probably an Aramean, or, as has been suggested, he may have been a son of the Judean royal house by an Aramean princess from Tabe-el.

In his fright Ahaz appealed to Tiglath-pileser for aid. The Assyrian moved quickly, taking advantage of the confused situation. He sent his army first down the coast, taking the Philistine plain and placing a blocking force against any Egyptian intervention. Then he conquered and took away from Israel all of Galilee and Transjordan, and moved from the rear against Damascus, which he laid waste. All conquered territory was reorganized as Assyrian provinces, ruled by Assyrian governors. Thus by 732 B.C., Israel was left as little more than a city state around the hill country of Samaria. She had kept that much independence only because someone named Hoshea murdered Pekah, took over the Israelite throne, and paid tribute to Assyria (II Kings 15:30; 17: 1-3). Judah and Jerusalem were saved, but at the expense of becoming a vassal of Assyria.

The biblical story of Ahaz represents him as surrendering his country's faith for the religion of his conquerors (II Chron. 28). In any event, he had to go to Damascus to pay his homage to the Assyrian monarch, and he had to continue that homage by the use of a special altar set up within the Temple precincts in Jerusalem (II Kings 16:10-16). For Judah it was a period of religious syncretism, and we learn from Isaiah that all sorts of foreign practices and superstitions were introduced, together with social and moral decay.

From a realistic point of view it now seems that if Ahaz had done anything else but surrender, his country would have suffered as severely as did Israel. Isaiah, as we shall see, interpreted the Assyrians as instruments of God's judgment against Israel and Judah. It seems probable that he indeed advocated a policy of nonalignment against Assyria. At the same time, the instability and complete lack of faith and courage on the part of Ahaz caused him to throw himself at Tiglath-pileser's feet and open his country to every policy, internal and external, that betrayed it. Nonalignment with Assyria, as well as with Israel and Damascus, would have involved payment of tribute but not the abject surrender of faith and morality. The Israelite prophet Hosea speaks of this period as a time when Israel is "like a dove, silly and without sense, calling to Egypt, going to Assyria"; it is "a cake not turned"; "they sow the wind, and they shall reap the whirlwind" (Hosea 7:11, 8; 8:7).

In less than a decade, presumably with the backing of Egypt, Israel again foolishly revolted. In 724 B.C., Shalmaneser V of Assyria sent his army and destroyed every remaining city, with unimaginable horror, as we may surmise from the excavation of such places as Shechem, Tirzah, and Dothan. The highly fortified capital, Samaria, held out for some time, and the Assyrian forces simply surrounded it to starve it into surrender. Finally, just as a new Assyrian monarch, Sargon II, came to the throne in the winter of 722-21 B.C., the city gave up, and Sargon claimed the victory for himself. He says that he took into exile 27,290 people. In the years that followed, people from various parts of Assyria were settled in the land. Israel as a kingdom was at an end, utterly ravaged, with most of its population killed (see II Kings 17).

The Later Years of Isaiah

The later prophecies of Isaiah, including much of chapters 1, 28-33, and 36-39, derive from the reign of Hezekiah. The biblical sources are confusing regarding the date of this king's reign. If, however, we take II Kings 18:13 seriously, to the effect that the invasion of Judah by the Assyrian army under Sennacherib in 701 B.C. occurred in the fourteenth year of Hezekiah (contrast II Kings 18:1, 9-10), then this king must have begun to reign about 715 B.C. The historical appendix to the collection of materials related to First Isaiah in chapters 36-39 (taken from II Kings 18:17—20:19) indicates that Isaiah was a well-known figure in the royal court and evidently an intimate of the king.

Hezekiah was a very different and much stronger person than his father Ahaz. He undertook a major national reform at a time when the Assyrian emperor, Sargon, was kept very busy with revolts and yearly campaigns to hold his empire together. The only Assyrian campaign into Palestine in this era appears to have been in 711 B.C. when the revolt of Ashdod, the chief Philistine city-state along the coastal plain, was crushed. Isaiah 18 and 20, and perhaps 14:28-32, are related to this event. Of particular significance for the national hopes was the revolt of Babylonia, led by Merodach-baladan, with the result that for more than a decade Sargon had no control over the southern Mesopotamian giant which a century later would supplant the Assyrians.

We are told of Hezekiah's sweeping reforms in II Kings 18: 3-6 and II Chronicles 29:31. Since the Northern Kingdom had been destroyed and Assyria appeared preoccupied, the political side of the reform included the reunification of Palestine under the Davidic dynasty in Jerusalem. Visions of the Messiah, the new king whom God would provide as savior, were seen and gave a fresh impetus to the Messianic hope (Isa. 9:2-7; 11:1-9; Micah 5:2-4). Whether the national hopes and the plans of Hezekiah were in any measure frustrated by Sargon, we do not know. What we do know is that at Sargon's death in 706 B.C. many parts of the empire revolted, and it was some years before the new emperor, Sennacherib (705-682 B.C.), got matters under firm control. Among those who revolted was Hezekiah, who led a coalition of the small states backed by Egypt, and to judge from II Kings 20:12-19 and Isaiah 39, backed also by the king of Babylon, who for a brief period about 703 B.C. again established his independence. In the north the Phoenician cities led by the king of Tyre were also involved.

Sennacherib responded in strength in 701 B.C., moving first against Tyre. With its surrender he quickly moved down the coast into Palestine, crushing the revolt. In his own version of the campaign he says: "As for Hezekiah, the Judean, he did not submit to my yoke. I laid seige to 46 of his strong cities . . . and conquered [them] . . . I drove out [of them] 200,150 people . . . Himself I made a prisoner in Jerusalem, his royal residence, like a bird in a cage . . ." Hezekiah surrendered in time to save Jerusalem, though he had to pay a heavy tribute which Sennacherib describes as "30 talents of gold, 800 talents of silver, precious stones, antimony, large cuts of red stone, couches [inlaid] with ivory . . . his daughters, concubines, male and female musicians." The biblical story says that Hezekiah paid three hundred talents of silver and thirty of gold, stripping both the royal and the Temple treasuries to do so, and even including the gold leaf from the doors of the Temple (II Kings 18:13-16).

These actions of Hezekiah brought him into sharp conflict with the prophet Isaiah. Playing the international political game was not Judah's mission in the world. To Isaiah it was a violation of all faith in God as Sovereign of world history to enter into foreign alliances. Assyria was God's agent (Isa. 10:5-19) for the time being, and the nations which were in revolt were in rebellion against God. The agreement with Egypt for revolt was "a covenant with death," a bed "too short to stretch oneself on it" (28: 15, 18, 20). " 'Woe to the rebellious children,' says the LORD, 'who carry out a plan, but not mine; and who make a league, but not of my spirit . . . who set out to go down to Egypt, without asking for my counsel' " (30:1-2). "The Egyptians are men, and not God; and their horses are flesh, and not spirit" (31:3). "For thus said the Lord GOD, the Holy One of Israel, 'In returning [repenting] and rest you shall be saved; in quietness and in trust shall be your strength' " (30:15). Yet the people are rebellious and say to the prophets, "Prophesy not to us what is right; speak to us smooth things, prophesy illusions" (30:10). In chapter 1, which appears to date from the Sennacherib period, Isaiah points to the consequences of the Assyrian campaign as God's judgment on a faithless people.

The events at the end of the reign of Hezekiah are not very clear. A number of historians have argued that Sennacherib must have led a second campaign against Judah a decade or more after his first one. If so, then we are to read II Kings 18:17— 19:34 and Isaiah 36-37 as referring to the second campaign. While the historical passages are perhaps somewhat ambiguous with regard to this question, the later prophecies of Isaiah are more easily understood if two Sennacherib invasions are assumed. The reason is that there are two groups of passages which say opposite things about what is to happen at the hands of the Assyrians. The prophecies which seem clearly to date from the time of Hezekiah's revolt in 705-701 B.C. denounce the king's action and the Egyptian alliance, as we have noted, and pronounce disaster for it as the decision of the heavenly court. In the midst of the revolt, the prophet at times appears to counsel surrender. On the other hand, there is a group of sayings which announce that God is going to deliver Judah and Jerusalem from the hands of the Assyrians, and that disaster is going to fall upon the latter (14:24-27; 17:12-14; 29:5-8; 31:4-9; 37:22-35).

Isaiah's prophecy that God would not destroy Jerusalem was evidently remembered over a century later and was taken to mean that the safety of Judah lay in its Temple, for God would not destroy his own house! This became the slogan of the priests who in 608 B.C. called upon the people to rally around the Temple for their safety. At the risk of his life the prophet Jeremiah publicly called this program a lie and a delusion, and in its place called for complete national reform as the only ground of safety (Jer. 7). Isaiah's divergent attitudes with regard to Assyria are not easily reconciled unless a second and disastrous campaign of Sennacherib, already suggested on other grounds, is presupposed. It seems clear that the remarkable deliverance of Jerusalem which Isaiah announces as God's decision is probably not the salvation purchased from Sennacherib in 701 B.C. by payment of a huge tribute.

OUTLINE
ISAIAH 1-39

Introductory Prophecy. Isaiah 1:1-31

Editor's Superscription (1:1)
The Indictment of the Nation (1:2-20)
Concerning Jerusalem (1:21-31)

Prophecies Regarding Judah and Jerusalem. Isaiah 2:1—12:6

World Peace in the Kingdom of God (2:1-5)
The Day of the Lord (2:6-22)
The Coming Social Chaos (3:1-15)
The Women of Jerusalem (3:16—4:1)
Jerusalem Purified (4:2-6)
The Vineyard of the Lord (5:1-7)
Laments Over the Evildoers (5:8-23)
"His Hand Is Stretched Out Still" (5:24-30)
The Call of the Prophet and the Syro-Ephraimitic War (6:1—9:7)
"His Hand Is Stretched Out Still," Concluded (9:8—10:4)
"Assyria, the Rod of My Anger" (10:5-19)
"A Remnant Will Return" (10:20-27b)
The Enemy Is at Hand (10:27c-34)
The Messiah and His Work (11:1-16)
Songs of Praise and Trust (12:1-6)

Prophecies Against Foreign Nations. Isaiah 13:1—23:18

Concerning Babylon (13:1-22)
Fall of the King of Babylon (14:1-23)
Destruction of the Assyrian Army in Palestine (14:24-27)
"Rejoice Not, O Philistia" (14:28-32)
Lament Over the Destruction of Moab (15:1—16:14)
Fragmentary Prophecies (17:1-14)
Message to Ethiopian Ambassadors (18:1-7)
Concerning Egypt (19:1-25)
The Prophet's Acted Sign of Egypt's Destruction (20:1-6)
"Fallen, Fallen Is Babylon" (21:1-10)
Disaster Coming to Arabian Tribes (21:11-17)
Exultant Jerusalem in 701 B.C. (22:1-14)

COMMENTARY
ISAIAH 1-39

INTRODUCTORY PROPHECY
Isaiah 1:1-31

Editor's Superscription (1:1)

This verse by an early editor identifies the author and gives his date by Judean kings of the second half of the eighth century B.C. Since Isaiah's call to prophesy came in the year that Uzziah died (6:1), the earliest prophecies are probably not before that date (about 734 B.C.; see Introduction). The prophecy is here called a "vision." In 2:1 the editor calls it a "word" which the prophet "saw." The prophets were primarily concerned with the "word" of the Lord which is heard. An age-old understanding of the manner of divine revelation in the biblical world, however, was that the gods made themselves known directly in dreams and nocturnal visions. In Hebrew prophecy the visionary and auditory terms have simply become a technical language for direct revelation. Even when "vision" is used, the content is nearly always a word spoken and heard.

The Indictment of the Nation (1:2-20)

Prophetic books frequently begin with a direct quotation of the message the prophet has received from the divine court, unless a biographical or autobiographical statement of the circumstances of the prophet's call precedes the prophecy itself. Here we are provided with one of the great statements of the prophetic message. Verses 5-9 indicate that the country had been laid waste by an enemy before the words were spoken. This suggests that the invasion of the Assyrian conqueror, Sennacherib, in 701 B.C. had taken place. Nevertheless, the passage is placed first because it states so eloquently what the prophet was called upon to speak in God's name to his people.

In verses 2-3 the words of God's indictment which the prophet has heard are quoted. As witnesses of this charge God calls the "heavens" and the "earth," meaning all of God's angels in heaven who were thought to be his ministers in his government of the world and all the inhabitants of the earth. The form of speaking is very old, going back to international treaties of the second millennium between an emperor and a vassal. The gods of the two parties were given as witnesses of the covenants, and the listings of divine names often concluded with the summarizing terms "heaven and earth," referring to all the gods of the two regions. When a treaty was broken, the divine witnesses were called to hear and to sustain the accusation against the vassal.

It is from this background that Israel derived the form which Isaiah here poetically uses. It means that God's Covenant with Israel has been broken, and God summons the witnesses to his treaty to hear his indictment: "Sons have I reared . . . but they have rebelled . . ." This is an action of supreme folly; it is contrary to nature; it is simply beyond rational understanding. Animals know their owners and the stables where they love to go for food and care, "but Israel does not know . . ." (vs. 3).

Having quoted God's solemn and frightening indictment, the prophet in verses 4-9 laments his people's present situation and explains the reason for it. "Ah" (vs. 4) here translates the Hebrew word used in a funeral lament, which may also be rendered "alas" or "woe." That is, a tragic situation exists which is to be deeply lamented: "a people laden with iniquity . . . have despised the Holy One of Israel." The last phrase is a title for God which is a favorite one with both First and Second Isaiah. In verses 5-8 the devastated nature of the country is described; it is a badly beaten and wounded body. The inference is clear: the rebel people have been punished for their breach of a most solemn treaty. God mercifully saved the lives of some; otherwise the nation would have been wiped off the face of the earth as Sodom and Gomorrah had been in Abraham's time (vs. 9; Gen. 18-19).

In verses 10-20 the prophet quotes in more detail the words of God's indictment. Do the people not know that God is disgusted with their worship in all its forms? He wants no more of their sacrifices and offerings; he can no longer endure their services of worship, for they weary him; he will no longer listen or hearken to their prayers because of their bloody hands. If they wish God to pay attention to their religious rites and to find their worship pleasing to him, let them wash themselves. Let them remove their evil, seek justice for the weak and defenseless of their society, learn the good, and cease the many forms of oppression whereby the strong enlarge themselves at the expense of the weak.

The traditional understanding of verse 18, as though it were a promise of mercy, can no longer be made to fit into the structure of the divine indictment. The context is the explanation of God's will and purpose for Israel and his conditions for blessing and for safety in the land. If they obey their Ruler, they will indeed prosper; but if they rebel, they will suffer. This is God's decree; this is the way of safety. In this context verse 18 is to be understood as follows: "Come, now, let us present our cases as though we were in a court of law [such is the meaning of "reason together"]: If your evil deeds are like scarlet, are they going to be judicially deemed to be white as snow? If they are as red as crimson, can they be white as wool?"

The background and basis of this prophetic declaration is Israel's understanding of what God wanted in the Covenant society and of his reasons for forming the nation of Israel and giving her a land as her responsibility. These involved the whole life of the nation as a people *of* God and *under* God. Whether it was political, economic, or social life, every phase of it must reflect their commitment to God's will. Since the people of Israel had once been slaves in Egypt, they understood God's righteousness as involving a special love and concern for the defenseless and poor of the nation. Hence Israel's whole social and economic life could be said to be a response to God's command to "love your neighbor as yourself" (Lev. 19:18).

God's indictment, however, is that Israel's society is in violation of the very reason and purpose of its existence in the world. In such a situation do the people think that their various rites of worship are going to make their history safe for them? It is characteristic of mankind to elaborate a great religious cultus, participate in it actively, and then assume that the divine world should respond by providing security and prosperity in the earth. Yet in Israel, God will have none of this kind of worship. Temple rites and services are good in themselves, but God finds them acceptable only when used by sincere people whose other actions and the society they have created reflect their commitment.

Concerning Jerusalem (1:21-31)

The remainder of chapter 1 consists of the declaration of

God's judgment against Jerusalem. Verses 21-23 are a lament
over the city's moral condition, and verses 24-26 present God's
decision to be a refining fire, after which she will be restored indeed as "the city of righteousness." The door to hope is only
through the purifying fire. The theme of judgment continues in
verses 27-31. Verses 29-30 contain a play on words: certain
paganizing rites are referred to with regard to oaks and gardens,
and the people of Jerusalem are going to be like an oak or a
garden without water, so that it withers.

PROPHECIES REGARDING JUDAH AND JERUSALEM
Isaiah 2:1—12:6

In these chapters, provided by an editor with a new superscription (2:1), most of the prophecies appear to come from an
early period in Isaiah's ministry. One section (6:1—9:7) is largely
in prose and contains biography (7:1-3) and autobiography (6:
1-8), and its background appears to be the events of 734 B.C.
(6:1; 7:1-6). This small booklet seems to have been inserted into
the midst of a group of prophecies arranged in 2:6—5:30 and
continuing in 9:8—10:4. That these groups were once continuous
is suggested by the refrain in 5:25 which is repeated in 9:12, 17,
21, and 10:4. The beautiful portrayal of world peace in 2:2-4
is quoted from another source; it appears also in Micah 4:1-4,
where the final lines of the poem, omitted in Isaiah, are preserved
in verse 4. Chapter 12 also quotes from ancient hymns of praise,
the dates of which are unknown. The prophecies of judgment in
9:8—10:34 are followed by passages in chapter 11 which declare God's marvelous purpose of salvation and restoration following the judgment. It seemed to an editor that the proper place
for the hymnic fragments in chapter 12 with their assurance and
joy in the Lord was at this place, before the prophecies against
foreign nations which begin in chapter 13.

World Peace in the Kingdom of God (2:1-5)

For singular beauty of thought and word, for profundity of
theological understanding and simple grace of expression, the
eschatological passage in 2:2-4 is unsurpassed in Scripture. At

this point Jerusalem as the capital of a political state in the eighth
century B.C. is left aside, and in its stead there is the vision of the
New Jerusalem which is the spiritual capital of the whole world.
This is an eschatological passage in that it presents the picture of
God's intention, that is, of the direction of history toward the
Kingdom of God. "Kingdom" in this sense means, as it does
generally throughout Scripture, world order established through
universal acknowledgment of the rule and sovereignty of the God
who chose Jerusalem as the place where he revealed his nature
and intention in history.

The passage begins by saying that in the great days to come
the hill on which the Temple in Jerusalem rests will be raised to
become the highest of mountains, and people from all over the
world will stream toward this central point. They will do so because there God has chosen to make his will and way known
for all mankind. In the bitter disputes between nations and peoples, and in the selfishness of the human lust for power, God
out of Zion has made known his Word and his Law. When all
people acknowledge this fact, and when God becomes the Judge
who decides the issues between nations, then will come peace—
and only then. Then the weapons of war will be turned into agricultural tools, and none shall learn war any more. (For a concluding verse to the hymn, see Micah 4:4.) A world without war
and without fear—this is a world in which all men acknowledge
the sovereignty of God, his will as made known in Jerusalem,
and in which the lust for power is disciplined in the commitment
to the universal Sovereign of all men and nations.

In the past most interpreters have tended to think of this
beautiful passage as dating later than both Isaiah and Micah. Being anonymous, it was inserted by the disciples of Isaiah and by
those of Micah along with the prophecies of their masters. In
terms of contemporary research, however, it is just as likely that
the passage could be older than both prophets and was quoted
by them in their own work, or included in their work by disciples. One small hint that this may be the case is the interesting
phrase "none shall make them afraid" which is contained in the
last verse, preserved only in Micah. The earliest datable occurrence of this phrase is in Isaiah 17:2, a passage that dates before
the destruction of Damascus by the Assyrians in 733-32 B.C. In
the other occurrences of this phrase, and in the way that it is
used, one can reasonably assume that its original context was in

the hymn, meaning that it is earlier than 733 B.C. An argument
based upon this phrase alone is insufficient to prove an early
date of the hymn, but it is indeed suggestive. In any case, the
hymn comes out of the liturgies concerned with Jerusalem as
used in the worship in the Jerusalem Temple. Verse 5 and Micah
4:5 are exhortations which adapt the quoted hymn to the context
of each prophet's own proclamation. Since what is said about the
way of the future is God's own promise, the meaning of it for
God's people in the present world is well expressed in the words
of verse 5: "Come, let us walk in the light of the LORD." The
direction of the future is clear; the issue now is the question of
God's sovereignty.

The Day of the Lord (2:6-22)

The prophet here speaks in his own words, explaining why
God has rejected his people (vs. 6) and is determined on punishing them. Verses 6-9 depict the situation in the nation. The people
have adopted such a variety of foreign manners and customs
that there is no health in them: magic and divination, playing
the game of militarism, and worshiping what their own hands
have made. By this means they have been "brought low" (vs. 9).
By this rejection of the very purpose of their being, Israel can
look forward not to prosperity but to terror (vss. 10-17). "For
the LORD of hosts has a day against all that is proud and lofty . . .
and the LORD alone will be exalted in that day" (vss. 12, 17).
At that time the idols of men will be cast forth as of no value
because they cannot save (vss. 18-21). Then at the end of the
section, in verse 22, an epigrammatic saying has been appended
containing a pessimistic appraisal of human beings generally.

Israel, caught within the imperialism of great powers, is here
called upon to look within herself for the cause. The nation is
to be torn asunder, and he who would grasp the meaning of the
terror must look to the righteousness of God, to "the terror of
the LORD." The same Lord who will in his own time establish
world order and peace without fear (vss. 2-4) is also the one before whom the haughty worshipers of themselves, the proud who
have created their own gods, must now stand in fear, "for the
LORD of hosts has a day . . ." (vs. 12)! The language and thought-
forms are derived from the old conception in Israel of God the
Sovereign in his role as commander-in-chief of the armies of the

universe. In the time of Moses and Joshua he used Israel as his
agent against evil powers. But now he will use foreign powers to
carry out the sentence against his own peculiar people. "The day
of the LORD" was in Israel an old expression for the day of the
Lord's victory in battle against his foes. In Amos 5:18 we have
the first use of the expression in prophecy. There, as here in Isaiah, God's victorious day will not be victory for Israel. It will
instead be a day of terror, for God's own people have become
his enemy, and therefore are the object of his punishing action.

The Coming Social Chaos (3:1-15)

In the coming disaster, law, order, decency, and leadership will
come to an end. Food, water, and leaders will be no more (vss.
1-3). Boys will be government officials ("princes," vs. 4), and
oppression will be the rule (vs. 5). The whole people will be in
anarchy (vss. 6-12); indeed, their leaders have misled and confused them.

For this reason God has entered his courtroom to bring formal
charges against his nation for their Covenant violation (vss. 13-
15). He has entered his legal brief against the elders and government officials, making against them this charge: they have crushed
the poor and have used the poverty and defenselessness of the
weak as their source of wealth and strength.

The Women of Jerusalem (3:16—4:1)

Yet the fault does not lie only with the leaders in Jerusalem.
Their women are every bit as bad and will suffer terribly in the
days to come. They will be widowed and humbled until as many
as seven will beg a man to marry them to give them a home and
protection (3:25—4:1). In the ancient world the lot of a widow
was certainly not to be envied. She had no independence of action such as is the case today; she had no life unless attached to
a household.

Verses 18-24 give one of the most detailed listings from the
ancient Near East of the fine attire worn by wealthy women of
court society. It is unfortunate that we cannot be sure about what
the terms all mean, except that the prophet's meaning is perfectly
clear. These irresponsible society women will suffer in the coming

day, for they, too, have been completely heedless of the purpose
of their lives.

Jerusalem Purified (4:2-6)

A beautifully written prose passage of God's future intention
of salvation is abruptly inserted in the midst of prophecies of
judgment, as though to relieve the tension and to lift the eye
from the immediate terror to the future. From what context the
disciples of Isaiah or the Isaiah "school" obtained this small piece
we have no way of knowing. Nor can we reconstruct the precise
reasons for its being inserted at this place.

It serves the purpose, however, of describing the real reasons
behind God's punishment. God's judgment on a people for betrayal and evil is not simply for the sake of punishment alone.
As stated in verse 4, it is to wash and cleanse the inhabitants of
Jerusalem from the blood and filth of their lives. When that
cleansing is completed, then God will make his continued presence known to his people as he did in the days of the wilderness
wandering of Israel from Mount Sinai. He will appear over
Mount Zion in the form of a cloud by day and a flaming light
by night (vs. 5; see Num. 9:15-23). In the same verse the cloud
and flaming fire are also called "glory." In the traditions of the
Jerusalem priesthood the glory of the Lord was a remarkable
and vivid symbol of the Lord's presence in the midst of his people. While the person of God himself can never be seen because
he retains his mystery, he nevertheless reveals his "glory" as the
sign of his presence. This is a particularly eloquent way of speaking about the known reality of God's presence, but it prevents
materialization of that presence as was done with the gods of
polytheism who were mysteriously present in their idols. God
preserved his mystery, but in his grace he was present among
his people.

The setting of this passage within a context of the prophet's
pronouncements of judgment and suffering upon Israel indicates
something of the ground of Israel's hope. In the midst of history
there is suffering and death because of evil and betrayal. Yet
because of the knowledge of the ultimate goodness of God, life
and hope spring up in the wreckage of the human hope of earth.
Out of death comes life; this is a basic biblical theme, central to

the prophets, and, of course, summarized and given new point in the cross of Christ in the New Testament.

The Vineyard of the Lord (5:1-7)

This is an unusual passage which forms a striking parable, but at the same time it is introduced as though it were a popular love song. The first line, "Let me sing for my beloved," calls to mind the love poetry in the Song of Solomon. It may be that during the fall festival which celebrated the completing of the wine harvest such popular songs were commonly sung, and that Isaiah was using the form of such a song as a way of fitting his prophecy into a given context of a great festival. At the same time what the prophet has to say in the song is a very bitter word. The subject is about a vineyard which was planted with great care but which would produce nothing but wild grapes. In verses 3-4 the prophet asks his hearers what he should do with a vineyard that responds to his care and careful ministrations in this manner. In the final section of the poem (vss. 5-6) the speaker and poet says that he will destroy the vineyard; because it is so unfruitful it will again become a waste. Then in verse 7 the prophet thrusts the lesson home with an abrupt explanation of what he has been really talking about. This vineyard is the house of Israel on whom the Lord has lavished such care and attention. But when he expected justice to come from the vineyard, there was instead bloodshed; when he had the right to expect the fruit of righteousness, he instead heard a cry from those who were oppressed. In the Hebrew there is a powerful play on the words translated "justice . . . bloodshed" and "righteousness . . . cry" which brings the song to a very quick and abrupt conclusion. The sin of Israel is her perversion of the good. For love and care she has returned infidelity. The implication of the song, therefore, is clear: the people of God in their vineyard of the Promised Land will be destroyed as a useless vineyard would be destroyed by the vineyard keeper. One perhaps can imagine the prophet himself singing this song as a way of making his prophecy to an assembled audience. Or if he did not sing it himself, then he would have had some popular singer present it.

Laments Over the Evildoers (5:8-23)

This section includes the first series of the prophet's "woes" over the people of Judah and Jerusalem. It has generally been supposed that the prophetic "woe" is an imprecation, meaning in effect, "May God bring woe upon people who act in this or that evil manner." The Hebrew word translated thus is, however, a simple exclamation which would be better rendered "alas." In everyday usage it was used at the death of someone, or in a comparable situation of grief or tragedy. A prophet killed by a lion was laid in a grave and people "mourned over him, saying, 'Alas, my brother!' " (I Kings 13:30). Jeremiah says that Judeans will not lament for the wicked king, Jehoiakim, saying, "Ah [alas] lord!" (Jer. 22:18). The prophet's "woe" thus is to be interpreted as a form of lament. Wicked people are those over whom the prophet could utter a funeral lament. They were people to feel sorry for because the judgment of God would soon fall upon them. The "woe" had the effect of announcing the judgment, and its mood probably held a considerable element of irony. Only in very late times when the term was followed by the preposition "to" or "upon" can one say that the lament form had come to be conceived as a direct statement of God's judgment upon given individuals.

The first of Isaiah's "woes" in verses 8-10 is a lament for those who by every means, legal or illegal, buy up field after field until there is no room in the land for any but themselves. The prophetic word was always addressed to the leaders of the society, to the strong who controlled public policy and whose actions so affected the weak as to make them weaker and poorer. In the oldest legal traditions of Israel the leading people of the nation were warned not to make poverty an opportunity for profit (see Exod. 22:25-27). Speculation in land was frowned upon because it tended to deprive the weak of the means of making a livelihood. God owned the land, and he had given it to Israel as to a steward. In theory, therefore, there should be no private ownership with the power to buy and sell the land in perpetuity (Lev. 25:23). Consequently the Jubilee Year was devised, when land would revert to the original clan to which it had been allotted by God (Lev. 25:8-17). This institution was too impractical to be put into legal and regular operation, but it shows the depth of the concern for the poor. Isaiah's words about the amassing of landed property by the wealthy rests on old Israelite tradition which regarded such a situation as a subversion of the Covenant society.

The next "woe" concerns the irresponsible use of wine and

strong drink. The tradition of Israel had no thought that the
wrong lay in the vine or in its products. Rather the wrong lay in
the people who made the excessive use of alcoholic beverages a
substitute for social responsibility: "they do not regard the deeds
of the LORD." It is this irresponsibility in the use of property and
in private life which in verses 13-17 is indicated as the reason for
the coming exile of the people from the land God had given them
in trust. Sheol, the realm of the dead, is pictured in verse 14 as
a hungry animal with mouth stretched open to swallow the great
ones of Jerusalem. Their death is the humbling of the haughty
that the Lord of Hosts may be "exalted in justice" (vss. 15-16).

Verses 18-19 picture the Covenant violators as people who
draw sin along behind them as a cart is drawn by ropes. Then
they plead ignorance of the way of the Lord and ask that God
make speed that his purpose may be known. The remaining verses
of the section (vss. 20-23) further summarize in vivid expressions those for whom lament must be uttered. They are those
who turn all values around, calling "evil good and good evil,"
putting "darkness for light and light for darkness." They are very
wise in their own eyes and very valiant at strong drink, but they
"acquit the guilty" and "deprive the innocent of his right." Indeed, the problem is just that: subversion of responsible society
by irresponsible actions of the men who have the power to affect
the lives of others.

"His Hand Is Stretched Out Still" (5:24-30)

The collectors of Isaiah's prophecies inserted at this point a
group of poetic sayings about the coming judgment of God, each
of which seems once to have concluded with the refrain: "For
all this his anger is not turned away and his hand is stretched out
still" (vs. 25). The group is continued in 9:8—10:4. The two
sections seem to have been split apart for the insertion of 6:1—
9:7, a short scroll containing pieces of autobiography, biography,
and prophecy from the time of Isaiah's call about 734 B.C.

Verses 24-25 picture the coming devastation of the land as
though it had already happened because the people had rejected
God's Law and despised his Word. The refrain means that the
judgment is not at an end; the directing hand of the divine Sovereign is still raised in command; God's agents of punishment
will continue their work. The agents are an enemy "nation afar

off" which growls and carries off the prey and "none can rescue"
(vss. 26-30). Yet the violation of the divine order is so great that
more than historical forces are unleashed. It seems as though the
whole natural order also is in convulsion, so that mountains
quake (vs. 25) and land and sky are in darkness (vs. 30). The
society that despises justice despises also the sovereignty of God
and refuses the obedient service which is his due. A world so
alienated cannot have peace and security. It will instead hear the
constant growling of preying animals, and there will be darkness
over the land and distress.

The Call of the Prophet and the Syro-Ephraimitic War (6:1—9:7)

It is with these chapters that one could very well begin the
study of Isaiah after the completion of the first chapter where
one learns of the identity, office, mission, and message of the
prophet. The date of Isaiah's call "in the year that King Uzziah
died" (6:1) and the events in 7:1-17 and 8:1-18 appear to have
been closely bound up in one another (see Introduction). The
call from God to his prophet happened at a time of international
crisis. At the end of Uzziah's life, when his effective leadership of
the west against Assyria had ended because of his illness, and
during the first year of the reign of his son Ahaz, in 734 B.C.,
Jerusalem and Judah were threatened with the loss of independence. Ahaz was a weak man who refused to have anything to do
with the western coalition against the Assyrian emperor, Tiglath-
pileser III. He was then attacked by the northern kingdom of
Israel and by the kingdom of Damascus, and to save his throne
he gave away his country's independence by offering it with heavy
tribute to Tiglath-pileser. What he tried to save he gave away. It
was at the beginning of this series of events that Isaiah received
his call and commission. In response to the situation and in its
setting the prophet provides us with two of his best-known passages: the sign to Ahaz (7:10-14) and the first datable prophecy
of the Messiah (9:2-7).

Isaiah's Call and Commission (6:1-13)

The call and commissioning of Isaiah take place in a vision.
In verses 2-4 the prophet sees the Lord enthroned in his heavenly
temple with mysterious winged beings called "seraphim" minister-

ing to him and forming an antiphonal heavenly choir. As is the case with all dramatic theophanies in the Old Testament, there is a shaking of the foundations, an opaqueness as of smoke (or in the darkness a brilliance as of fire) which prevents the prophet from seeing the person of the Lord directly, and there is the hearing of a great voice (vs. 4). The personal circumstances of the prophet when he had this inward vision are unknown. It is often assumed that he was attending a great service of worship in the Jerusalem Temple. This, however, is a pure guess, because the prophet says nothing about where he was or under what circumstances the vision came. It is certain, however, that his vision concerns God in his heavenly court, and not in the earthly Temple, as verse 8 makes clear. In the background of the vision, however, there is a definite auditory element: the heavenly choir singing antiphonally, "Holy, holy, holy is the Lord of hosts; the whole earth is full of his glory" (vs. 3). The holiness of God is an attribute which Isaiah stresses. When we in our churches today sing the well-known hymn, "Holy, Holy, Holy," which is derived from this verse and vision, we are to think of the majesty, the exaltation, and the mystery which belong to God and to God alone. Holiness is that ineffable quality that originates in God himself and differentiates him from all of his creation. People and temple on earth can be said to be "holy" only in a derived sense, meaning that they are closely related to God himself. The Israelite did not know what God's person or being was like. God is the ultimate mystery of power, direction, and meaning in the world. It is in the contemplation of this holy, ineffable, and powerful mystery which man cannot control but on which he is utterly dependent that reverence and worship begin. The words of the heavenly choir, therefore, are words of worship in which the Object of worship is magnified and glorified, and the whole of the creation is acknowledged as being filled with God's "glory"; that is, with the revelation of himself. In this context the word "glory" is used in a larger sense than it is in the particular usage in 4:5.

The prophet's reaction to his vision of God's holy majesty leads him to a devastating sense of his own unworthiness and that of the people among whom he lives (vs. 5). The sense of God's holy perfection brings confession to his lips. Indeed, it may be said that true confession of one's inadequacy is only possible when the perspective of one's seeing is altered by the vision of God. Confession, however, is followed immediately by the sacrament of forgiveness (vss. 6-7). The burning coal from the altar fire touching the lips of the prophet in his vision is a symbol of purification to him and he hears the words, "Your sin [is] forgiven."

Only when the purification of the lips and the assurance of forgiveness are present, are the ears of the prophet opened so that he can hear a discussion going on in the heavenly court. A decision has been reached by the court, and the Lord is now asking his angelic assistants who it is that will bear the message of the court to those on earth who are affected by it. At this point the prophet himself answers boldly, "Here am I! Send me." God accepts the prophet's offer of himself and appoints him to the office with the word, "Go." That is, the great religious experience which comes to the prophet does not have a mystical purpose wherein the experience of God's reality is itself the central meaning of the event. Rather, it is that the prophet may be changed in his way, so that he has a new path to follow and a commission from God himself; that is, he has a job to do as the mediator of God's Word to the people.

God's commission to Isaiah is that he bear a terrible message to the people of Israel. The words in verses 9-10 must be understood to be purposive hyperbole which has the aim of shocking people to pay attention. The words are ironical. If we listen to them as addressed to us, the irony becomes clearer: "Hear, but do not understand; see, but do not comprehend. Let your hearts be fat, your ears heavy, your eyes shut, lest you see, hear, and understand and repent and receive the healing mercy of God." The purpose is to say forthrightly that God's decree of judgment has been issued and the time is now far gone. When the prophet asks in despair, "How long, O Lord?", God replies that it will be until the land is utterly laid waste and the people are exiled from their former homes (vss. 11-13). Even though a tenth of the former population may remain, it will again suffer. The nation is to be nothing more than a felled tree of which there remains only a stump.

This is Isaiah's first announcement of a "remnant" of the nation which will survive. In his early prophecies this remnant is not a sign of hope; it is a sign of judgment. There will be nothing more to the nation than this remnant. A prophet editor adds the final word from a later time, when the remnant has become a source of hope that in the time of suffering there will indeed be survivors—namely, the true Israel, refined and purified by God. Such would appear to be the meaning of the words at the end of verse 13, "The holy seed is its stump."

As the reader may note from the footnote in the Revised Standard Version, the ironic nature and the disturbing directness and terribleness of the words coming through the prophet in verses 9 and 10 are used by Jesus according to all four of the Gospels, as well as by the Apostle Paul, in situations where the refusal of people to hear and take heed made the words appropriate.

Isaiah and King Ahaz (7:1-17)

The dramatic incident related in this section appears to have been written by one of Isaiah's disciples, since in verse 3 the prophet's name is mentioned and the story is related in narrative fashion. The attack of the two kings on Ahaz of Jerusalem has so frightened King Ahaz and his people that they are said to have shaken "as the trees of the forest shake before the wind" (vs. 2). At a time when the king was inspecting the open canal which brought water from a spring into the city, God sends Isaiah out to meet him. One of the problems in defense of ancient cities was that of providing a certain supply of water for the inhabitants within the city walls during a time of siege. Portions of an old aqueduct which lead to a pool at the southern end of the hill Ophel from the Gihon spring in the Kidron Valley have been discovered by archaeologists. So also has the city wall around the city in the time of Isaiah. The wall was low enough along the slope that we may understand the aqueduct to have been inside it for protection.

For the first time we hear of one of Isaiah's sons: the prophet is told to take him along to his meeting with the king while the latter is inspecting the aqueduct. The boy's name is given as "Shear-jashub." It seems clear that the boy was to accompany his father because his name presented one of the main points of Isaiah's early prophecy: the name meant "a remnant shall return." As previously indicated, after disaster had befallen Judah, the prophecy of the remnant would be one of hope. At this stage in Isaiah's career, however, it was one of judgment, and is to be interpreted, "only a remnant shall return."

God's message through Isaiah to the king is simply that he

"Take heed, be quiet, do not fear" (vs. 4), because God's decree is that the attack upon Judah will not be sustained or successful. The implication of verses 8-9 is that both Damascus and Samaria are shortly to be destroyed. A parenthetical statement inserted by an editor at the end of verse 8 is difficult to interpret. It speaks of sixty-five years as the period within which the northern Israelite kingdom will be broken to pieces. Actually, the destruction of Israel occurred in two stages, in 733-32 B.C. and in 724-21 B.C. (see Introduction). The final and complete destruction of Samaria occurred in the second of the two periods and is described in more detail in II Kings 17.

In the second part of verse 9 Isaiah uses a play on words in his description of God's message to Isaiah which he, the prophet, is called upon to convey to the king. In Hebrew it is one short poetic line in two parts with three words in each part. The first part of the line, "If you will not believe" (or "be sure"), refers to the king's faith in God. If he will not commit himself completely to God in faith and in trust, then certainly he is not going to be firmly established or secure on his throne in Jerusalem. The Hebrew word used in the word play is a verb which is one of the primary terms in the Hebrew vocabulary for faith. "Believing," in this context, does not refer to an intellectual acceptance of an idea, but to a complete and entire commitment of the self to God so that in whatever crisis one finds himself, he can stand firm in confidence in the faithfulness of God. If the king does not have this commitment, but instead trembles in fear as though God did not exist, then of a truth his security on the Jerusalem throne is threatened.

As a way of confirming his faith, Ahaz is instructed to ask a sign of the Lord, that is, some unusual happening or event in order to confirm the king's wavering faith. Ahaz very piously and unconvincingly gives the classic answer to such a request: it is not proper to put the Lord to a test of this type (Deut. 6:16). In reply, Isaiah says that the Lord will provide a sign (vs. 14). It will be a most unusual and remarkable event. A young woman shall bear a son and name him "Immanu-el," meaning "God is with us." The exact significance we are to place on this passage is not clear, because the meaning is not elaborated. The main point of the sign is an assurance that indeed God is with his people. Judging from 9:6 and Micah 5:2-3, however, it seems clear that the Jerusalem and Judean prophets of the eighth century were speaking of a birth of a new child of the royal line who would be God's answer to the problems of the present era. That is, God would provide the new king who would carry out all of his promises. The reason that such an event would be spoken of in terms of the birth of a new royal child would seem to be a special way of calling attention to a dramatic intervention of God in the human scene. There are three birth stories of this nature in the Bible. They are those of Moses, Samuel, and Jesus. In each case the birth of the child is God's answer to the need of the present moment. It is God's new and dramatic act of grace for the salvation of those in trouble. In this context it is not surprising that the otherwise rather enigmatic verse 14 should early have been considered as a Messianic prophecy and that Immanuel would be one of the names of the Messiah to come.

Matthew 1:23, following the Greek translation, refers to this passage as being fulfilled by Jesus Christ and translates the Hebrew word in question as "virgin" instead of "young woman." The exact history of how this interpretation came to be made cannot be traced, but virtually all modern interpreters who have studied the question say that the Hebrew word in question refers to any young woman of marriageable age and does not in itself require the translation "virgin." There is another Hebrew word which has the unequivocal meaning "virgin."

The remainder of this section in verses 15-17 is by no means as clear as an interpreter would like it to be. The main point is certainly in verse 16. That is, before the child reaches the age of discernment the coalition of the two kings who are threatening Ahaz with war will have broken up and the threat to Jerusalem will have come to an end. Verse 15 probably is to be interpreted as meaning the same thing, but the Hebrew is simply not clear. Verse 17 continues with the promise that the Lord will bring great things upon Judah and upon the dynasty of King David in Jerusalem, things such as had not happened since the division of the kingdom of David into two parts, as narrated in I Kings 12:1-20. The final words of the verse, "the king of Assyria," is a later addition, apparently by an editor who knew what indeed had actually happened. The overriding single fact of ancient Near Eastern history between the ninth and seventh centuries was the power of the Assyrian empire and its conquest of one small state after another, forcing them all under a burden of heavy tribute.

Prophetic Fragments Concerning the Coming Terror (7:18—8:10)

This section is apparently not a continuous prophecy, but rather a series of fragments, all concerning the coming disaster. Verses 18-20 refer to the terror activities of the imperialistic powers, Assyria in particular. In verses 21-22 the reference to "curds and honey" seems to suggest the reversion of the land to a pastoral state in which these foods of the semi-nomadic dweller with his flock will be the staples of the land, rather than the foods grown ordinarily by agriculturists. Verses 23-25 continue with the same theme: the settled and the agricultural land will return to a place for the grazing of cattle and sheep. It perhaps should be noted that these words are not a mere pessimism on the part of the prophet. What he states here actually did take place in the destruction of Samaria and the cities in the central hill country by the Assyrians in the period 724-21 B.C. While Judah received a severe punishing at the hand of the Assyrian, Sennacherib, in 701 B.C., the complete destruction of all settled occupation of the land was not to come until a little over a century later at the hands of the Babylonians (587 or 586 B.C.).

The paragraph 8:1-4 returns to the theme of the war against Ahaz in 734 B.C. Here we learn of a second son of Isaiah with a very long name, Maher-shalal-hashbaz. Again it is a symbolic name referring to one of the major points in the prophecy which Isaiah is called upon to deliver to his people. The name means "speed the spoil, hasten the prey"; that is, it refers to the coming destruction of Damascus and Samaria, as verse 4 makes clear. As was the case with the prophet Hosea, so the private life of Isaiah is used to dramatize and symbolize the dreadful message which the prophet is called upon to deliver to the people.

A new prophecy in verses 5-8a is closely related to the foregoing. The metaphorical reference in verse 6 to the "waters of Shiloah" is to the waters of the aqueduct to which allusion is previously made in 7:3. The meaning is that because the people cannot trust in the quiet waters, a great river, the river of Assyria, will sweep over its banks and overflow into Judah. Politically this means that the forces let loose when Ahaz in his frantic fear appealed to Assyria for aid will not stop with the destruction of Damascus and Samaria, but will sweep over and engulf Judah also, which indeed was the fact.

The second part of verse 8, "its outspread wings will fill the

breadth of your land, O Immanu-el," is most easily understood
if it is read with the lines of poetry which follow in verses 9-10.
This would appear to be a fragment of a hymn of hope and
praise to God, though the antecedent of "outspread wings" is
not here preserved. The reference, however, must be to the wings
of God that will cover the land as a protection so that all those
who attack the country will fail, "for God is with us." Here a
play on words is again used wherein "Immanu-el" is addressed
directly in verse 8b, but the meaning of the name is translated at
the end of the poetic fragment. Since the country of Judah is
referred to as "your land, O Immanu-el," there is an additional
suggestion that Isaiah's Immanuel prophecy in 7:14 is indeed
meant to refer to the new king whom God is going to supply as
salvation to his people.

Autobiographical Fragment (8:11-22)

Chapter 8 continues in verse 11 with autobiographical material from the prophet, but in this case the word of the Lord is
addressed to him personally and contains advice and counsel as
to how he should act in the present crisis. The time still appears
to be early in the prophet's ministry. Indeed, the "conspiracy"
mentioned in verse 12 is probably that of the Syro-Ephraimitic
War of 734 B.C. Verse 11 speaks of the Lord's "strong hand
upon me," a vivid expression of prophetic inspiration. The
prophet understood himself to be in the grip of One who was
stronger than he, so that his whole self was caught up in concentration upon God and his will (see also Ezek. 3:14). In
verses 11-15, Isaiah, and presumably with him his disciples, is
told to separate himself in attitude and spirit from the society
in which he lives. The will of God is going to be a stumbling
block both to Israel and to Judah, and many people are going
to stumble upon it and be broken. Their separation and alienation
from the true purposes of God is so far advanced that there
seems little hope for them (compare 6:9-13). Consequently,
Isaiah's standard of attitude and conduct must not be drawn
from among the people but from God alone. The words "fear"
and "dread" in verse 13 are common Old Testament words for
religious reverence, upon which all worship depends. They do
not refer to groveling fear before the Lord, except in passages
that refer to evil people who may expect or are experiencing
the dreadful judgment of God. From this point on into the New

Testament the call for separation from the main social group
which is thought to be in deep error becomes more and more insistent. From now on the true Israel of God is not necessarily
the nation. God's activities will be directed toward the creation
of the true Israel.

Verse 16 is the first reference to disciples of a prophet and
their relation to the prophecy. Isaiah is told to seal up his
prophecies among his disciples so that they can preserve them.
Meanwhile Isaiah himself is to wait patiently for the Lord to act
in fulfillment of what he has said to his prophet, while he and
his children in their going out and in among the people will continue to be signs of the prophecy already uttered (vss. 17-18).
The prophet's work is over for the moment, and he must now
wait upon the Lord to act, entrusting his message to his disciples
for preservation.

Verses 19-22 again give a picture of the state of the people
now and in the days to come. At the moment they are inclined
to turn to spiritualists and mediums, as though it were proper
to consult the dead on behalf of the living. God has made his
will known by his teaching and testimony, and it is most strange
that the people should prefer the practices of paganism to the
clarity and simplicity of the manner in which God has revealed
himself to them. As a result, in the days of the coming judgment
they will be enraged and disillusioned with king and Temple, but
when they look about themselves they will see only darkness and
distress.

The Messiah: God's Light in the Darkness (9:1-7)

The hymn in verses 2-7, concerned with the Messiah and the
Messianic age, is one of the most familiar and beautiful of the
Isaiah prophecies. Verse 1 is a prose introduction which gives
the setting and the date of the poem in the view of the prophetic
editor of the material of Isaiah. Following 8:22, with its picture
of the darkness of the earth, 9:1 presents another abrupt shift to
a glorious future. This historical reference to the land of the
tribes of Zebulun and Naphtali is to be understood in connection
with the campaign of Tiglath-pileser III in 733 B.C. which took
away from Israel all of Galilee and turned it into an Assyrian
province. The end of the verse refers to the caravan highway
across Galilee; the last phrase should be understood as referring
to the course of the highway "from the land beyond the Jordan

to Galilee of the nations." In the days to come Galilee will be restored and made glorious. The implication of the verse is that while Galilee had been removed from Israel by the Assyrians, Samaria itself had not yet fallen as it was to do between 724 and 721 B.C. Thus, at least in the view of an editor, the hymn which follows refers to the same events as does most of the material in chapters 6-8.

The first section of the poem (vss. 2-3) refers to the transformation which has come over the people who were in darkness. The light has shined upon them and there is great joy. The second section (vss. 4-6) gives the reasons for the joy, each of the three verses being introduced with the same word. First the rod of the oppressor has been broken as on the day when Gideon defeated the great Midianite invasion (Judges 7). The remains of battle equipment (vs. 5) are burned. Then at the climax is the announcement of the birth of a royal son on whose shoulder the government is to be placed and whose name will be composed of four titles of God himself. "Wonderful Counselor" refers to him who is all-wise in his plans and purposes. "Mighty God" refers to the Lord as a great warrior who cannot be defeated. "Everlasting Father" refers to God's fatherly relation to and care for his people. "Prince of Peace" refers to more than God's purpose to maintain a world without war. The Hebrew word for "peace" is much richer in that it includes within it also the concept of a harmonious and wholesome existence. These titles are commonly read as describing the character of the Messiah, although it was a common custom that children should be named with reference to God. In this case the child will bear a series of names which refer to the nature of God himself. In that way a special relationship between God and his king is indicated. The Messiah is the instrument of the purposes of God referred to in the titles.

Verse 7 promises the permanence of a government of peace and justice in the kingdom ruled from the throne of David forever. The final poetic line states that all of this will be accomplished by the zealous activity of the Lord of the armies of the world.

Christians have always read this passage as referring to Jesus Christ, and the words have become very familiar, not only from their frequent use in the Christmas season but also from their musical setting in Handel's *Messiah*. Christ indeed was the fulfillment of the purpose of God as expressed here. To the people

of Judah and Jerusalem, however, the words would have had
their own meaning in the Judean context, unillumined by the
fresh perspectives given to them in the New Testament.

The author of this poetic prophecy was one who was very
familiar with the theology of monarchy as it had been elaborated
in the Jerusalem court beginning in the time of David and Solomon. This theology centered in the understanding that God had
made an unbreakable promise to David that a member of his
dynasty would always reign in Jerusalem (see II Sam. 7:8-16).
The Davidic king, therefore, in the Jerusalemite theology was to
be the instrument of God's government over Israel and, in the
great day to come, over the whole world. Psalms 2 and 110 are
understood today to be among the hymns sung in Temple services where this theology of monarchy was being affirmed and
God was being praised for his promise and purpose.

In the course of time, however, God's promise to the Davidic
dynasty was the occasion of query among some of the people,
for different reasons. When the nation was in trouble, people
could wonder whether or not God would keep his promises. The
certainty that he would do so was the faith that people could
hold on to in time of crisis (see Ps. 89). Few kings of either
the Northern or the Southern Kingdom, however, reigned in
accordance with the will of the Lord. And so the promise, as in
Isaiah 9:2-7, shifts the theology and the promise in the Davidic
covenant from the reigning king, in this case Ahaz, to a king
whom God is about to provide. The theology of monarchy thus
becomes less a description of what the office of the reigning king
then was than a promise of what God would make it in the days
to come.

In this context some interpreters today view verses 2-7 as a
hymn or oracle composed by Isaiah or someone else to celebrate
the accession of an actual Judean king. The words in verse 6,
"For to us a child is born," are taken either as a reference to a
"child-king," or as a metaphorical reference to an adult king's
becoming a "son" of the Lord by adoption on the day of his
anointing. If such a view is correct, then we must understand
that Isaiah himself or an editor of the Isaianic prophecies has
used the hymn for a slightly different purpose than that for
which it was originally composed.

A difficulty with the interpretation just given, however, is the
announcement of the birth of a child which is followed immedi-

ately by the statement about God's government to be realized
through that child. This type of thing is, as far as we know, not
the common formula used for kingship in the ancient Near East.
A much simpler and less forced interpretation is to read the
words in connection with the setting of 6:1-9. That is, in the
darkness of 734 B.C. and in the weakness of King Ahaz, God
through his prophet takes the occasion to announce the forthcoming fulfillment of his promises of old. He himself will raise
up the king in whom he will fulfill his promises. In both 7:14
and 9:6 the manner of that new event begins in the birth of a
new royal son. We have noted that in the three birth stories of
the Bible which are given us in some detail (Moses, Samuel, and
Jesus), each story signified the dramatic intervention of God at a
critical juncture. Similarly here, the statement of the birth of a
child is the sign of a new mighty act of God in the salvation of
his people.

"His Hand Is Stretched Out Still," Concluded (9:8—10:4)

This section concludes the collection of prophetic oracles begun in 5:24-30 which was interrupted by the special scroll 6:1—
9:7. Four prophecies in 9:8—10:4 (9:8-12, 13-17, 18-21; 10:
1-4) all end with the same refrain, to the effect that God's action
in the judgment of Israel is not yet at an end. The prophecies,
therefore, date before the final destruction of Samaria in
724-21 B.C. The first (vss. 8-12) speaks of God's raising up adversaries against Ephraim and Samaria, though we do not have
sufficient information in detail to be sure of the exact historical
reference. The second prophecy (vss. 13-17) speaks particularly
of the leaders of Israel, both the elders and the popular prophets
who teach lies. These will be cut off in the judgment. The third
prophecy (vss. 18-21) suggests the inner social and political
chaos then existing inside the nation of the north during the last
days of its earthly life. Finally, 10:1-4 is a prophetic lament comparable to those in 5:8-23 about the leaders of the nation who
used positions of power and trust, in particular the law, as a
means of defrauding the poor of the country of their right so
that the latter became a prey.

"Assyria, the Rod of My Anger" (10:5-19)

The greatest imperialistic power of the world in Isaiah's time was Assyria, with its capital at Nineveh. The dreadful use of the military power of the Assyrians was felt in every country in the ancient Near East from Persia to Egypt for a period of nearly three hundred years, until it decayed from within and was conquered from without by the Medes and the Babylonians in the period between about 630 and 609 B.C. In these verses Isaiah reveals God's purposes in using this mighty military force. It was inconceivable to a Hebrew prophet that the Assyrian empire could have been created and maintained had not the sovereign Lord of the universe so decreed. It was thus the prophet's task to explain to his people what God's intention was. In so doing, Isaiah by implication gives in brief statement the prophetic view of history.

The passage begins in verses 5-6 with a lament, introduced by the Hebrew term which is translated "woe" in 5:8, 11, 18, 20, 21, and 22. In the ancient world, at the time of a death or of any national or local disaster it was felt to be proper to utter a lament over the sad event. The prophets in using this form turned it into an effective way of announcing the coming of God's judgment upon the people or nation thus lamented. The only clue to the date of this lament over the future fall of the Assyrian empire is in verse 9. Damascus was destroyed by Tiglath-pileser III in 733-32 B.C. The Assyrian conquest of the other cities mentioned in the verse was probably in the period between 722 and 717 B.C., that is, early in the reign of the emperor Sargon II (722-705 B.C.). An Assyrian army was investing Samaria in the winter of 722-21 B.C. when Sargon came to the throne. The Syrian cities revolted and were reconquered by Sargon in the succeeding years. It is not unlikely, therefore, that this passage also derives from the early period of Isaiah's prophecy. It interpreted to the people of Judah the meaning of these Assyrian conquests and the future of Assyria herself shortly after the fall of the northern kingdom of Israel.

Verses 5-6 assert that the Assyrian military power is the instrument of God's judgment, for so the "anger" of God should be understood. The use of the human emotions of anger and jealousy in relation to God is the Hebrew way of expressing most vividly the active displeasure of God against that which

thwarts his will. In no case, however, are these terms to be understood as suggesting that God is ever acting outside the bounds of
his righteous and redemptive purpose.

Verses 7-11 explain the problem and essential idolatry of the
great militaristic power. He does not have the intention of being
an agent of God. He has one thing in mind, and one only: to
destroy and strike fear into the hearts of Jerusalem and Samaria.
His threat, then, is that he will do to Jerusalem what he has
done to Samaria (vs. 11).

An editor seems to have supplied verse 12 as an explanatory
comment on the text of the poem. Isaiah's meaning, he correctly
states, is that when the Lord has finished the punishment of
Jerusalem he will then turn on the arrogant boasting of the king
of Assyria. Verses 13-14 continue verse 11, where the Assyrian
monarch is explaining what he is doing. He says that by his own
strength and by his own wisdom he has removed boundaries and
gathered the treasures of the earth. Isaiah sharply draws the
conclusion in verses 15-16. Shall the axe deem itself greater and
more important than the person who uses it? Quite the contrary!
Because of the self-idolatry of the great power, the Lord of the
armies of the world will in due time strike down the conqueror.
In verse 17 the "light of Israel" and "his Holy One" are to be
understood as names for God, who will become a fire which will
burn and devour the Assyrian army until there remain so few
that a child could enumerate them (vss. 18-19).

Assyria and similar world powers of course do not understand
that they are simply agents. They are interested only in world
domination, and for their own iniquities in due time they will be
punished. God's use of a historical instrument for the accomplishment of his purpose does not confer righteousness upon that
instrument. Not even the greatest of the militaristic powers of
history have done their work outside the context of God's purpose and control. Empires have risen and empires have fallen,
and the Lord's will has both been done and violated.

This is a realistic view of history in relation to the sovereignty
of God. The meaning of history and man's hope do not lie in
the possibilities within the human soul to expand and develop
for itself a glorious future. Neither do they lie in the Marxist
supposition that the inexorable movement of history toward the
classless society in a conflict of the "haves" and the "have-nots"
is somehow built into the very constitution of things, so that the

ideal age will inevitably come about as soon as the capitalist class
is removed. To the biblical writer such views would be idolatrous.
The meaning of history and the hope of man lie only in the
consistent purpose of God himself, a purpose which always
stands over history as it is being unfolded within history. For
this reason, in the darkness of any particular moment of time
one can live by faith and hope in the providence of God.

"A Remnant Will Return" (10:20-27b)

At this point an editor has placed some prose fragments derived from original prophecies of hope. The kingdom of Israel
has been destroyed. Isaiah has foretold this event, and one of his
sons, Shear-jashub (7:3), was a further prediction of it in the
meaning of the name, "[Only] a remnant will return." Now that
the disaster has fallen, this prophecy becomes a ground of hope.
Indeed a remnant *will* return. In verses 22-23, however, the original oracle against Israel is preserved and consequently the original meaning of the teaching regarding the remnant. Verses 20-21
and verses 22-23, when put together in this manner, make explicit the two uses of the doctrine of the remnant. Yet they
surely come from different periods in the prophet's ministry.

Verses 24-27 are addressed to the people in Zion, that is,
Jerusalem. They are not to be afraid of the Assyrians, for in a
short time the oppressors will be destroyed and the yoke removed from the neck of the Judean people. It is possible that
this prophecy comes from the end of Isaiah's ministry and belongs with a group of sayings which announce that God is going
to deliver Judah and Jerusalem from the hands of the Assyrians
and that the Assyrians will meet disaster. It is possible that they
refer to a disastrous campaign of the emperor Sennacherib
about 690 B.C. (see Introduction).

The Enemy Is at Hand (10:27c-34)

This is a vigorous portrayal of the advance of an enemy
through the tribal area of Benjamin just north of Jerusalem to
the village of Nob, which was probably located on the high ridge
directly east of Jerusalem, known in the New Testament as the
Mount of Olives. The investiture and siege of Jerusalem is about
to begin.

Commentators have generally taken this to be a picture of the advance of the Assyrian army on Jerusalem. Yet the Assyrians usually came down the coastal plain, and in 701 B.C. they attacked Judah and Jerusalem from that area. The Babylonians did the same in 598-97 B.C. and again in 588-87 B.C. It is quite possible, therefore, that the attack pictured in these verses is that of the combined forces of Israel and Damascus in their attack on Judah in the attempt to force Ahaz into their coalition against Tiglath-pileser III in 734 B.C. (see Introduction and 7:1-17).

Verses 33-34 do not belong with verses 27c-32 but are an independent prophecy of judgment against either Israel or Judah or both. In this case the Lord is represented as a forester who cuts down great trees, as, for example, those on the Lebanon Mountains to the north.

The Messiah and His Work (11:1-16)

Chapter 11 is composed of two main sections: verses 1-9, concerned with the Messiah, his inspiration and his work; and verses 10-16, concerned with the Messianic age and the regathering of the exiled peoples of Israel and Judah from among the nations. The materials in the chapter thus deal with eschatology, that is, with the ultimate future for which, by faith, the people of Judah and Jerusalem could hope after the coming judgment and purification had taken place. Other passages of similar import are 2:2-4; 4:2-6; 9:2-7; and 10:20-21.

The beautiful prophecy of the Messiah and of the Messianic age in 11:1-9 should be studied along with 9:2-7. In neither of these passages is the actual term "Messiah" used. It was, however, the theological title of the Davidic king in Jerusalem, and meant "anointed," referring to his induction into office by the holy oil of anointing, so that it was understood that he was especially separated in his office to a particular work to be done in behalf of the Lord. Contrary to a common belief, Messianic passages are very infrequent in Old Testament literature; that is, if the term "Messianic" is applied strictly to those prophecies having to do with the king of David's line whom God will provide as leader of his people and with the new age on earth which will arrive with the new king. Of course, the people of the Dead Sea Scrolls and the New Testament writers will see events of their times fulfilling in remarkable ways a variety of passages

in various contexts of the Old Testament. Yet, historically, the
promise of the new king in the line of David whom God will
provide in the eschatological age will be found only among the
Judean prophets who are very familiar with the theology of the
Davidic monarchy and with the promises of God to David. The
chief of these passages are those in Isaiah 9 and 11, and Micah
5:2-4. There are other references, but not as central to the
prophecies, in Jeremiah and Ezekiel. In the postexilic period,
references will also be found in the prophecies of Haggai, Zechariah, and Malachi.

Verses 1-3 describe God's king as a branch growing from the
stump of Jesse, that is, from the family of David's father. He
will be empowered by the "Spirit of the LORD" and also with
such enlightenment and strength of character as will be necessary for him to accomplish his great work. Yet "his delight," indeed his whole concentration, will be upon his reverence for the
Lord—for so the term "fear" should be understood in such a
context as this. The term "Spirit of the LORD," called "holy
Spirit" in Psalm 51:11 and in the New Testament, is in the Old
Testament an agent sent forth by God to work within human
beings so that they may be enabled to do the work which God
calls them to do. It is thus an agency of the divine Government.

The second section extends from the middle of verse 3 to the
end of verse 5. These lines depict the manner in which the new
king will use his sovereignty. All that he does will be within the
context of his saving righteousness, his compassion for the weak,
the meek, and the poor of the earth, and his determination that
the strong and the powerful shall not oppress them. Indeed,
righteousness and faithfulness are said to be clothing that he
wears.

The final portion of the prophetic poem (vss. 6-9) describes
the radically changed situation in the world at that time when
God, through his righteous king, will actually be in charge of the
whole earth. In that day there will be a transformation of all life
so that the unhealthy and unnatural killing and destroying going
on among human beings and between human beings and animals
and between animals and other animals will come to an end.
Thus none shall hurt or destroy any more, "for the earth shall be
full of the knowledge of the LORD as the waters cover the sea."
The word "knowledge" here, as elsewhere in prophecy, does not
refer simply to a body of knowledge or factual data. It refers

rather to the acknowledgment of God's sovereign claim upon us and our glad willingness to follow wherever that claim may lead us. Of course, we cannot understand a world in which there will be no killing of animals for meat whatsoever. Yet the point of these lines is that they forecast the future peace of the whole of God's creation, the peace which can come only in our common allegiance. There can be no loving of neighbor and wholesomeness of heart between those of very different natures except in the context of a previous commitment and purification of heart in the sovereignty of God.

It is not entirely clear that the second part of chapter 11 forms one composition. Indeed, it would seem that there is a gathering together of fragments, not all of them of the same date. Verse 10 pictures the Messiah as a kind of flagstaff in the midst of the nations to which all peoples of the world will rally. The remainder of the chapter (vss. 11-16) portrays the new age as a time when the Lord will recover the remnant of his people, the outcasts and dispersed of Israel and Judah, from every part of the earth. Indeed, out of the Assyrian empire there will be as it were a special highway for the return of Israel (vs. 16), and their exodus will be comparable to that from the land of Egypt in the days of Moses. In spite of God's judgment, and his destruction of Judah, the grace of God is known and the people can hope. They will indeed have a future which God will provide because God does not lie. It is because of prophecies such as this that the Hebrews as a people survived the destruction of their nation and the annihilation of most of their brethren and remained a people of the Lord. The disasters that were to mean the death of the nations and of the nations' gods meant the survival of Israel and the deepening of faith and hope and loyalty.

Songs of Praise and Trust (12:1-6)

At this point, which is at the end of the first major section of Isaiah's prophecies, two fragments of psalms of praise are introduced (vss. 1-2 and 3-6). The origin and date of these psalms are unknown, yet in the editing of Isaiah's prophecies their insertion at this point is quite appropriate. In the terrible historical disasters which the Hebrew people in Palestine must suffer at the hands of the Assyrian army, and this as the judgment of God, there is nevertheless a future still to be hoped for in the Lord.

For this, God can be praised even in the darkness of disaster.
Verses 1-2, like many of the psalms in the Psalter, are a personal
expression of thanks, or rather praise, to God. Although the
psalmist had been in great difficulty he had trusted in God, he
was not afraid, and God had been his salvation. Such a personal
psalm when used in public worship would have expressed the
faith and trust of every member of the congregation who had
been in similar difficulty. The second psalm (vss. 3-6) has many
echoes in other psalms and hymns in the Old Testament. The
inexhaustible wells of God's salvation can always be drawn upon.
For this, the whole congregation is called to sing and shout for
joy, "for great in your midst is the Holy One of Israel."

PROPHECIES AGAINST FOREIGN NATIONS
Isaiah 13:1—23:18

All of Israel's prophets—at least in cases where considerable
material from them is preserved—were concerned about the
world situation, and it was a part of their calling to issue prophecies against the other nations in the civilized world of their day
(see Jer. 46-51; Ezek. 25-32; Amos 1-2). One explanation
not infrequently given in the past has been that the prophets were
intense nationalists and that their words against the nations were
simply a part of their own intense patriotism. According to this
view, consequently, it is improbable that we should look to this
material for much that is edifying to modern life. Such a view,
however, is scarcely adequate to the deeper and theological dimensions of the world view of the prophets. Their language is
filled with legal terms and legal conceptions. God is the sovereign
Ruler of the world of men, and he rules in the context of law
and order. God is not only the Sovereign of Israel and the One
who maintains the standards of order in Israel, but he represents
also the moral order of the world of men. Consequently, in Israel
international treaties and world organization were taken extremely
seriously. To Isaiah the various vassal treaties through which
Assyria ruled the greater part of the civilized world of the eighth
century B.C. were backed by the will of God. It was God's will
that for a time at least, the Assyrians should control the world.
When a treaty with its solemn oaths was broken, then one must
expect trouble. The divine Suzerain is he who maintains the
treaty made in accordance with his will, and he metes out the

appropriate punishment due at its breach. To comprehend the prophets' viewpoint we must take seriously their understanding of God's role as Suzerain of the world, a world which is bound together in various ways by law. God as the world's Ruler and Judge maintains world order. Most of the prophecies against foreign nations are against those which have joined Israel or Judah in revolt against the rule of a major power. The role of the current great power, however, is not eternal, but is limited to such time as God determines (see the comment on 10:5-19).

Concerning Babylon (13:1-22)

The editorial superscription to chapter 13 says that it is an "oracle concerning Babylon" and ascribes it to First Isaiah ("Isaiah the son of Amoz"). The term for "oracle" here, however, is generally used only in later prophecy as a term for a message announcing doom to a people. It literally refers to a "burden" which God intends for a people to bear. The only historical reference in the prophecy is in verses 17-18, where the Medes are being stirred up by God to bring an end to Babylon, which at that time is "the glory of kingdoms." For this reason the setting to which the prophecy is addressed must have been the period after the death of Nebuchadnezzar about 550 B.C. In the time of Isaiah, Babylon was not a great power; though for a brief time it had asserted its independence from Sargon II and from Sennacherib, it was weak. Like all other countries of the west in the second half of the eighth and first part of the seventh century, Babylon was a vassal of Assyria. Furthermore, though older prophetic material may have been used in this prophecy, the conception of universal destruction and the "return to chaos" theme is most typical of the latest period of prophecy, in the sixth and fifth centuries B.C. If we may speak of a "School of Isaiah" (see Introduction), then we can see the work of these disciples of both First and Second Isaiah in inserting certain anonymous prophecies in what were felt to be appropriate places.

In any event, what is pictured in this passage is a scene of war. The nations of the world are gathering together in a great "tumult on the mountains" (vs. 4); but the Lord is also mustering his armies for battle, for the Day of the Lord is coming (vs. 9) and the whole of the earth is to become a desolation. The primordial darkness (vs. 10) will be present and both heavens and earth (vs. 13) will tremble and shake. At that time the evil of the world and the haughtiness and ruthlessness of men will be done away. The Medes will be one of God's agents to bring to an end the great Babylonian empire (vss. 17-19).

The whole universe is here depicted as in convulsion because God is cleansing it of its evil. The reference to the cessation of light and to the shaking of the foundations is the type of theme which is common only in late prophecy and which belongs to what is usually called "apocalyptic eschatology." It deals with a return, or threat of a return, to the original chaotic situation before God created the world. This end of known history will come about before God's new day will dawn. Earlier prophecy tends to be more historically centered and to see things in the context of definite imperialistic armies.

Fall of the King of Babylon (14:1-23)

One of the most remarkably vivid and ironic dirges in the Old Testament appears in 14:1-23. Its theme is the fall of the king of Babylon, and its date therefore may well have been in the sixth century, like that of the poem in chapter 13. It concerns both the joy of those set free from their oppression, and at the same time their surprise that one who considered himself to be as powerful as any god could so quickly be brought low. Verses 1-4a form a prose introduction to the poem and speak of the Lord's release of captive Israel from the hands of others and of restoration to their own land. The pain and hard service allotted the people have come to an end. Verses 22-23 are a prose conclusion to the poem inserted by an editor or by a prophet so that the poem would be seen in the context of God's decree of the destruction of Babylon.

The first section of the poem (vss. 4b-8) is the statement that God has broken the power of the oppressor who ruled the nations with terror, so that now the whole earth is at rest and in song. Even the cedars of Lebanon rejoice because no conqueror is cutting the precious cedar wood for use in his palaces. In the second section of the poem (vss. 9-11) the scene changes to Sheol, the abode of the dead beneath the earth. There people who once were in life now exist as "shades" of their former selves. The former leaders of the earth rise from their thrones and exclaim in surprise: "You too have become as weak as we!" Thus their pomp is "brought down to Sheol."

In the third section (vss. 12-15) the poet uses some vocabulary from Canaanite mythology. Babylon is like Helal, the "Day Star," son of Shahar ("Dawn"). This minor star in the pantheon of the gods has tried to ascend to the height, to put his throne over all of the other gods in the "mount of assembly." The latter is the cosmic mountain in the far north which was thought in Canaanite religion to be the abode of the gods. Babylon is one who would establish himself as the suzerain of the whole earth, but he has fallen out of heaven to the earth and has been brought down into Sheol like any other man. The reference to "Pit" in verse 15 is here used as a synonym for the underworld. The remainder of the poem continues the same theme as something to be pondered: "Is this the man who made the earth tremble, who shook kingdoms . . . ?" (vs. 16). Such is the fate of all the lofty and the proud; they are brought low. Death is the great leveler of all the artificial distinctions which man creates upon the earth. At the death of this conqueror there is no glory. He has destroyed too many lands and slain too many people. As he killed in violence, so he will die in violence.

Destruction of the Assyrian Army in Palestine (14:24-27)

The brief passage in verses 24-27 is an authentic word of First Isaiah which deals with the destruction of Assyria, the world power of that day. Isaiah announces in God's name that it is the divine purpose that the Assyrian power will be broken "in my land." The passage is to be read with the other verses from the end of Isaiah's life which express God's decision to save Jerusalem (for example, 37:21-36). The two groups of passages in Isaiah, one group which proclaims God's decision to destroy Jerusalem and Judah, and the other smaller group which announces God's plan to save the city by the destruction of the Assyrian army in Palestine, are difficult to harmonize with one another, unless the second group refers to a second campaign of the emperor Sennacherib about 690 B.C. (see Introduction).

"Rejoice Not, O Philistia" (14:28-32)

The final verses of chapter 14 are exactly dated in the year of the death of King Ahaz; that is, about 715 B.C. At that time the people of the cities of Philistia located along the southern coastal plain of Palestine, where the Philistines had settled in the twelfth century B.C., are addressed by the prophet and told not to rejoice, for the time of their destruction is near and God has determined it. It would be better, therefore, if they were to wail in mourning.

The precise occasion for this prophecy cannot be known with certainty. Furthermore, textual problems in verse 32 make translation and interpretation of the concluding passage very difficult. The simplest hypothesis, however, is to read this passage together with chapters 18 and 20 as concerned with the Philistine revolt against Sargon II. This rebellion was led by the city of Ashdod, and presumably envoys had come to Jerusalem to seek aid in the forming of a coalition to rebel. Judah did not join the rebellion, and Ashdod was crushed by Sargon II in 711 B.C. If this interpretation is adopted, then "the rod which smote you" (vs. 29) may refer to Assyria and not to Ahaz. The latter was a weak king who indeed had been in battle with the Philistines, but they had been strong enough to wrest Judean territory away from him (II Chron. 28:18).

Lament Over the Destruction of Moab (15:1—16:14)

Among the prophecies against foreign nations in the prophetic books, Isaiah 15 and 16 are unusual in their beauty and in the depth of feeling expressed. Moab as a people with a monarchy was established on the plateau east of the Dead Sea in the thirteenth century B.C. During the twelfth and eleventh centuries it had expanded northward to the area directly east of the northern tip of the Dead Sea, having taken over the tribal area previously occupied by the Israelite tribe of Reuben. In the tenth century the country had become a vassal kingdom of David (II Kings 3:4-27), but it had been able to secure its independence shortly after 850 B.C. Most of the chief towns and geographical features of the country are mentioned in these two chapters, and the theme concerns their destruction. The whole country is to be laid waste, and in 16:9 and 11 the author of the lament expresses his own deep sorrow over what has happened.

The date, authorship, and context of this lament have occasioned considerable discussion. According to 16:13-14, the lament is something spoken concerning Moab in the past but now within three years the Lord has decreed its fulfillment. In the case of

Moab during the ninth and eighth centuries, insufficient information is available to enable us to determine the background of the
destruction in question. In 16:1-5 there is the suggestion that
some Moabites requested asylum in Judah, and 16:4-5 looks forward to the time when a new David will sit on the throne of Jerusalem and rule Moab in justice and righteousness. In the period
between 652 and 648 B.C. a great revolt against Assyria broke
out in Babylon, and apparently throughout the Assyrian empire.
Judah seems to have been involved, so that the Judean king was
summoned to Babylon (II Chron. 33:11). At that time Arabian
tribes of the Syrian desert overran the eastern settled lands of
Syria and Palestine. It may have been this event which marked
the end of Moab as an independent state. In any case the state
of Moab seems to have disappeared during the course of the
seventh century, and Isaiah 15-16 would appear to have been
a lament of an Israelite written for the occasion. Its conclusion
in the Isaiah literature indicates that it was considered prophecy
(16:13-14). Certain verses of the poem are used also in a lament
over Moab preserved in Jeremiah 48, although the latter lacks the
touch of emotion and compassion which is in Isaiah. In any case
there seems to have been a parent composition to which both
these laments go back, but the history of it is very difficult to
establish.

Fragmentary Prophecies (17:1-14)

Concerning Damascus (17:1-6)

Chapter 17 seems to be made up of a series of fragments, none
of which is necessarily complete in itself. The clearest is the first,
in verses 1-6, which is a prophecy of the destruction of Damascus
in 733-32 B.C. at the hands of the Assyrian emperor, Tiglath-
pileser III. According to verse 3, fortifications will be removed
from the northern kingdom of Israel and the kingdom itself will
disappear at Damascus, so that those who are left in Syria (the
kingdom of Aram) will be no better off than the people of Israel.
The context seems clearly to be the threat of the coalition of
Syria and Israel against Judah in 734 B.C.

Concerning Idolatry (17:7-11)

In this section (vss. 7-11) the main theme holding the material together seems to have been idolatry. On the one hand, in the days to come men will turn again to their true Creator and will worship no longer the things which their own hands have made (vss. 7-8). The "Asherim" is the name for cult objects in paganizing shrines which were symbols of the Canaanite mother goddess. In verses 10-11 there is reference to setting plants in a garden in honor of a Canaanite fertility deity. There will be nothing harvested from such plants; they will only bring pain. Note the parallel titles for the Lord in verse 10: "the God of your salvation" and "the Rock of your refuge." A people whose only security in the past has been in the Lord who has saved them repeatedly cannot expect security in the future when they turn to a variety of pagan customs which can have in them no saving, but only destructive, power.

The Roaring of the Nations (17:12-14)

The final section of the chapter (vss. 12-14) compares the noise of the peoples of the world to the roaring of the sea. The context for this passage would appear to be an attack on Judah by the army of the Assyrians with its various contingents of troops from vassal peoples. Isaiah prophesies that they will be blown away like chaff and that it will be done quickly. The probable date of this passage would be after 701 B.C., and probably in the same context with the group of passages for which a second campaign of Sennacherib has been suggested (see Introduction; compare also 14:24-27; 37:21-36).

Message to Ethiopian Ambassadors (18:1-7)

The breadth of the prophet's horizon is indicated by this lament addressed to the ambassadors of Ethiopia. Actually, these men represent the Egyptian Twenty-Fifth Dynasty, which after 714 B.C. was in control of Egypt. A new king is now on the throne in Jerusalem. His name is Hezekiah (715-687 B.C.), and the Egyptian government is urging Judah, Philistia (see comment on 14:28-32), and the other small nations of lower Syria and Palestine to revolt against Assyria. Isaiah, who had not wanted Ahaz to throw himself at the feet of Assyria in the first place, now is most emphatically against any kind of an alliance for revolt. He addresses the ambassadors, and through them the whole world, saying that the Lord will make known in due time when the overthrow of Assyria will take place. It is necessary, however, to wait on God's time. It is his decision that Assyria should now rule western Asia, and he will decide when the rule will cease (vs. 7; see 10:5-19). He it is who founded Zion (Jerusalem); he is the Lord of his people, and no alliances with other powers are necessary.

Such was Isaiah's attitude both in the revolt of 714-11 B.C.— in which the prophet's counsel seems to have been taken seriously, with the result that Judah took little part in the affair (see comment on 20:1-6)—and also in the great revolt in the early years of Sennacherib between 705 and 701 B.C., when Hezekiah was the leader of a revolt (see comment on 28:1—31:9).

Concerning Egypt (19:1-25)

As the prophet continues his survey of the international situation in order to observe what it is that God is doing, his attention is fixed on Egypt. In the preceding chapter he had addressed a message to the ambassadors representing the new Ethiopian Dynasty that took over control of the government of Egypt about 714 B.C. The signs of the time, which to Isaiah are the signs of the Lord's working, point to the destruction of Egypt. The poetic oracle in verses 1-15 is composed of three sections. The first (vss. 1-4) pictures the political and social chaos in the country, with brother fighting brother, until they turn to magic and primitive religious practices and finally to a dictator, "a hard master" and "a fierce king" (vs. 4). This reference may be the prophet's interpretation of the disorders in Egypt which led to the seizure of power by the Ethiopian Dynasty. This is not absolutely certain, because the drive of the Assyrian army through Palestine to the border of Egypt was precisely for the purpose of conquering their ancient rival on the Nile in due course. Shortly after the time of Isaiah the Assyrian plans were successful. Lower Egypt was occupied by the Assyrian army in 671 B.C. and Thebes, the center of Upper Egypt and the ancient capital of the country, was destroyed in 663 B.C. While it is possible that the prophecy against Egypt has the country's ultimate destruction at the hands of the Egyptian army in view, verses 1-4 could most easily be interpreted as referring to disorders in the country during the prophet's lifetime.

The second section of the poetic oracle (vss. 5-10) pictures the disaster that comes upon the nation when the Nile River has insufficient water for irrigation. Egypt is a country completely dependent upon the Nile to irrigate and fertilize its valley each year. Outside the valley to east and west stretches the desert with drifting sand. Whether in Isaiah's time there actually had been a bad year in Egypt which the prophet is here interpreting as the work of the Lord, or whether he is prophesying a future disaster, is unknown. It is typical of prophecy to see both historical and natural forces at work in the destruction of a country, because the forces and powers in both are but servants of the Lord to do his will.

The third section (vss. 11-15) makes reference to the famed Egyptian wise men and points to their complete inability to divine the purpose of the Lord against their country. Consequently, counselors and government officials share "a spirit of confusion."

The editors of Isaiah's oracles have appended to the primary poetic word against Egypt a number of prose fragments in verses 16-25, the origin and date of which cannot be determined with certainty. While verses 16-17 are quite negative and seemingly nationalistic with regard to the future of Egypt, verses 18-25 preserve one of the most remarkable expressions of responsible international understanding which the Old Testament contains. They envisage the conversion of Egypt and of Assyria, for the smiting of Egypt is for the purpose of their healing and conversion (vs. 22). In the great day to come, therefore, Egyptians and Assyrians, the great political rivals of ancient times, will mingle together and worship together. Israel will be associated with them, "a blessing in the midst of the earth," and the Lord will be heard to say: "Blessed be Egypt my people, and Assyria the work of my hands, and Israel my heritage" (vss. 24-25). Israel will now be a part of a larger community in fellowship with the Lord. Indeed, this union of all mankind in the service of God, also expressed in 2:2-4, is precisely that which is the center of the Christian hope for the earth.

The Prophet's Acted Sign of Egypt's Destruction (20:1-6)

Chapter 20 is a small section of prose biography by one of the prophet's disciples, comparable in type of material to 7:1-9. When the Ethiopian Dynasty in Egypt attempted to organize a

revolt of the small nations to the north of her against Sargon II
(see comment on 14:28-32), the Philistine city-state of Ashdod
along the southern coastal plain of Palestine became the focal
center of the revolt. Judah evidently took no part in the uprising,
with the result that she was spared when Sargon's army destroyed
Ashdod and crushed the revolt in 711 B.C. It was at that time
that Isaiah heard the Lord's command that he should walk naked
and barefoot "as a sign and a portent against Egypt and Ethiopia"
(vs. 3). The people of that country will be exiled, naked and
barefoot as was the prophet. The reference in the same verse to
Isaiah's walking this way for three years would seem to suggest
that throughout the period of the revolt, from 714 to 711 B.C.,
he counseled Judah and all who would hear that the Ethiopian
Dynasty of Egypt was a weak thing to trust for support against
Assyria. In this he was proved right, because the revolt was
easily crushed, though the destruction of the capital of Egypt,
Thebes, by the Assyrian monarch Asshurbanapal (about 669-630
B.C.) did not occur until 663 B.C., long after the death of Isaiah.
The prophet's action was an extreme one because it was supposed
to attract the attention of people, and at the same time the word
of explanation always accompanied the action so that the people
would know for what it stood. It was not God's will that the
connivings of Egypt at this time would succeed; she herself was
going down to defeat and disaster. For the present Assyria was
God's servant and agent, even though she did not know it.

"Fallen, Fallen Is Babylon" (21:1-10)

This oracle is generally believed to be an anonymous prophecy
about the fall of Babylon in 539 B.C. to Cyrus the Persian and
the troops of his empire to the north and east. An unknown
prophet describes the meaning of the event, as the Lord had
made it known to him in a vision (vs. 2). In an ecstatic state
he sees the coming of horsemen and he hears the watchman cry,
"Fallen, fallen is Babylon; and all the images of her gods he has
shattered to the ground" (vs. 9). The short prophecy was evidently preserved by the school of Isaiah and placed here among
the prophecies against foreign nations, although we have no
means of reconstructing the methods or the reason for inclusion.

Recently a strong argument has been advanced to date this
oracle in the period of the revolt of Babylon against Sennacherib

in 691-689 B.C., presumably with the aid of the Medes and Elamites (vs. 2). In this case the "plunderer" would be the Assyrian
military power, and the Judeans would be those represented as
urging on the Elamites and Medes in the hope of the successful
defeat of Assyria. The terrible vision of the fall of Babylon to
Sennacherib comes to the prophet, and with it a sense of deep
disappointment, because it meant the continuation of Assyrian
power. Babylon did fall to Sennacherib in 689 B.C.; he sacked the
city and took the statue of its chief god, Marduk, back with him
to Assyria. If this interpretation is correct, then the prophecy
could be a genuine oracle of Isaiah.

Disaster Coming to Arabian Tribes (21:11-17)

The second part of chapter 21 concerns localities in central
Arabia, east and southeast of Palestine: Dumah, Dedan, Tema,
and Kedar. The first oracle (vss. 11-12) is quite enigmatic, particularly as a voice is represented as calling to Dumah from Seir,
which is Edom to the south of the Dead Sea. Nevertheless, the
inquiry of the watchman suggests threatening danger. The following verses concerning other oases in central Arabia are quite
clear; these localities have been attacked and are in great
danger. The historical context of these brief prophecies is most
probably the Assyrian attempt to gain control of the trade routes
of central Arabia which passed through the oases in question.
Such information as we have indicates that this was done both
by Sennacherib (705-681 B.C.) and by his son and successor
Esarhaddon (681-669 B.C.). It is quite possible, therefore, that
these fragmentary pieces may have come initially from Isaiah
himself in the time of Sennacherib.

Exultant Jerusalem in 701 B.C. (22:1-14)

This oracle is given the enigmatic title, "concerning the valley
of vision." The identity of this valley is unknown; the title is
taken from verse 5. The prophecy, however, concerns a people
who are shouting with joy from the housetops (vss. 1-2) and are
enjoying great feasting and drinking, heedless of the consequences, saying: "Let us eat and drink, for tomorrow we die"
(vs. 13). To Isaiah this conduct is unrealistic and inexcusable:
"For the Lord God of hosts has a day of tumult and trampling

and confusion" (vs. 5). That is, the people of Jerusalem are joyous over something that has happened, while the prophet thinks that instead there should be "weeping and mourning" (vs. 12), for although the Day of the Lord has not yet fallen it will surely come (vs. 14).

In the time of Isaiah the one historical moment when these words would have their proper context would appear to be in the year 701 B.C., when King Hezekiah had saved Jerusalem from destruction by paying a very heavy tribute to Sennacherib after the latter's capture and reduction of the fortified cities of Judah. This is made more explicit in the reference to the military preparations for siege described in verses 8b-11. "The House of the Forest" was the armory built in Jerusalem by Solomon (I Kings 7:2; 10:17). The reference to the reservoir between the walls refers to the new provision for water supply within the city fortifications, to which a long tunnel was cut through the rock from the Gihon spring (see II Kings 20:20). This, the Siloam tunnel, is still in Jerusalem, where it provides an adventure for tourists who walk through.

Prime Minister Shebna of Jerusalem Condemned (22:15-25)

This exceptionally interesting passage does not really belong among the prophecies against foreign nations, as is also the case with verses 1-14. The prophecy concerns the steward Shebna who bears the title "over the household." That was the official title of the vizier or prime minister of the government in Jerusalem, the chief executive of the country after the king. It is a title that was also borne by Joseph in Egypt (Gen. 41:40), and it has been convincingly argued that both the title and office in the Jerusalem government were in some degree modeled on the office in Egypt. What precisely the offense of Shebna was we do not know. He was hewing out a tomb for himself, and he is condemned by Isaiah as a bad man who is to be thrust out of his office. It is highly probable that this tomb has actually survived in the cliffs by the modern village of Silwan, directly across the valley from where the old city of David once existed south of the present sacred area in the old city. Isaiah tells Shebna that a man named Eliakim will be his replacement in office; and he indeed it is who in the crisis with Sennacherib is in charge of negotiations (36:3, 11, 22; 37:2). Verses 20-24 give an important picture of the nature of the office and the authority attached to it. Verse 25 is an appended passage which seems to suggest that in due course Eliakim was also removed from office, but the verse is by no means clear. It is a later addition to the earlier prophecy.

Concerning Tyre (23:1-18)

One of the most remarkable peoples of the ancient world were the Phoenicians, who are the subject of this prophecy. Inhabiting the territory of modern Lebanon, these descendants of the old Canaanites turned to the sea and founded trading colonies all over the Mediterranean area, becoming indeed "the merchant of the nations" (vs. 3). The "ships of Tarshish" (vs. 1) were the ocean-going trading vessels of Tyre's commercial fleet, named from Phoenician metal refineries as far west as Sardinia and Spain. Here Isaiah announces the purpose of the Lord to bring this country, the capital of which was Tyre, into trouble, evidently referring to its subjection to a vassal status under the Assyrians. Ezekiel 27-28 is a comparable prophecy from the time of Nebuchadnezzar. Both are valuable literary sources contemporary with the great days of Tyre and the Phoenicians. Verse 13 seems to be fragmentary and is obscure. It is an editorial comment that probably refers to the long siege of Nebuchadnezzar against Tyre. Verses 15-18 predict a seventy-year period of decline for Tyre, after which all her commerce will be dedicated to the Lord. This small eschatological fragment about the future of Tyre is difficult to fix precisely into the known history of the country. In any case it, too, is an appendix to the primary poetic oracle in verses 1-12.

THE AGE TO COME
Isaiah 24:1—27:13

Chapters 24-27 are a short collection of materials referring to the great age to come when the alienation of the world will have been done away and God will have brought about the new age of peace and security in the earth. At that time there will be no more death (25:8), and the dead shall have been raised from the underworld to share in the joys of the new time in which God's purposes in his original creation of the world will have been fulfilled (26:19). These chapters seem to be an appendix to the earlier prophecies of Isaiah, just as chapters 34-35 are appendices to material mainly from the latter part of Isaiah's ministry (chs. 28-33). The date of the variety of passages contained in the appendix cannot be established with any certainty.

The Earth Made Desolate (24:1-23)

The first prophecy in 24:1-23 pictures the desolation of the whole earth. It employs the elements of the "return to chaos" theme, that is, a reversion to the situation before creation. The whole earth will be laid waste and all society completely disrupted because it is polluted and has violated "the everlasting covenant," presumably the covenant with Noah (vs. 5; see Gen. 9:1-17). In verse 10 the "city of chaos" refers to the city of Jerusalem, which has become a chaos.

Following this is a hymn of praise to the Lord, and a call upon the peoples of the whole earth to sing praise to the "Righteous One" (vss. 14-16). Yet at the end of verse 16 the prophet inserts a note of sorrow for the treachery that is in the earth. This portion of chapter 24 was surely drawn from a source different from that of the first thirteen verses.

In verses 17-20 the language of the "return to chaos" motif is used again, including the opening of the windows of heaven to allow the waters of the great deep to fill the space between heaven and earth (see Gen. 7:11). Even the sun and the moon (vs. 23) will be "confounded" and "ashamed," as though they were persons responsible for the corruption of the whole creation. The angels in heaven and the kings of the earth all will be punished for their part in the corruption (vs. 21). In other words, there is nothing in man's hope for earth that can be considered reliable or permanent, for there has to be a great purification of the whole of creation and the whole of society. This can be brought about only by God himself. Man's hope, therefore, must center only in the manifestation of the glory of God (vs. 23).

God Be Praised (25:1-12)

Verses 1-5 comprise a hymn of praise to God for his purpose to save the poor and the needy from "the blast of the ruthless."

The context is a victory over an unspecified enemy and an un-named city (vs. 2). It has been conjectured that this poem may have been drawn from an earlier victory hymn in which some great power was destroyed, though God had preserved his own people. Actually, however, the references are general, so that they become fitting praise of the Savior of the weak and the poor in any of the disasters of earth.

Verses 6-12 are a series of prose fragments. Verses 6-7 refer to the great Messianic banquet which will be held in the days to come for the whole people of the earth. At that time the Lord will have done away with the veil or covering that is spread over all the peoples of the earth so that they cannot really see and understand the meaning of history or of God's sovereignty. Another beautiful presentation of this great banquet for all men in the age when all will have been reconciled to God is found in chapter 55. In the New Testament the presentation of the Lord's Supper draws upon this theme, so that it becomes a banquet of the Kingdom preparatory to the banquet for all men which will be presided over by the Messiah.

In ancient Israel death was something to be dreaded because it removed one from life, where God was most active. It was only in the very late period between the Old and New Testaments that a few Jews began to express the certainty that even death would be conquered in the age to come. Here is a beautiful expression of this thought: Death itself and all sorrow and trouble will be taken away from the people of the earth (vs. 8). For this we can hope, for the Lord has decreed it.

Verse 9 expresses the meaning of it all: "Lo, this is our God; we have waited for him, that he might save us." The final verses 10-12 are a negative statement of the future of Moab quite different in tone from chapters 15-16, and probably deriving from the period after the destruction of Jerusalem in 587 or 586 B.C., when the peoples across the Jordan had taken advantage of their afflicted neighbor and had raided and robbed.

"Thy Dead Shall Live" (26:1-21)

Chapter 26 is a psalm of trust, praise, and meditation, in all probability with elements drawn from older material. In the great age to come the people of Judah can rest confident in their city of Jerusalem, knowing that the Lord will "keep him in perfect peace, whose mind is stayed on thee, because he trusts in thee" (vs. 3).

Verses 7-16 are a combination of prayer and meditation on the ways of the Lord with the peoples of the earth. In God's world it simply cannot be that his adversaries will triumph. "For when thy judgments are in the earth, the inhabitants of the world learn righteousness" (vs. 9). In verses 16-19 the conversation in prayer with God continues. The people of Judah are like a woman in childbirth, in pain but bringing forth nothing. At this point the sudden joyful exclamation appears in verse 19, concerning the resurrection of the dead. The conception is both social in that the restoration of the nation is probably in view (compare Ezek. 37), but also individual in that men of the past are to rise to share in the joys of the new earth. This is a conception which is rare in the Old Testament and flowers most vividly in the Intertestament period (see Dan. 12:2). Finally, in verses 20-21 the people living at the time of the psalmist are addressed directly. This picture of God's future means that in the coming days of terror God's people should hide themselves and be patient until the purification of the earth is accomplished. This is the type of theme that appears in the postexilic age after the destruction of Jerusalem. At that time it was realized that what prophets like Isaiah, Jeremiah, and Ezekiel had announced about the punishment of the Covenant nation had come about at the hands of the Assyrian and Babylonian armies. Now they are to wait until God's punishment of the whole world is complete, for only after that revolution will God bring in the new day.

"In That Day" (27:1-13)

Chapter 27 is composed of several fragments or short prophecies, with very little connection between them. Verse 1 is the most dramatic of them and is a very stirring symbol. Here allusion is made to the Canaanite creation myth in which one of the chief gods killed the dragon of chaos symbolized by turbulent waters of the sea, or else by a great serpent or dragon in the sea. Here in a prophetic context it refers to the dragon as no longer a symbol of the chaos of nature, but rather as a symbol of the evil of the world in defiance against God. In God's final day his triumph over the dragon thus is a symbol of his triumph over all forces of alienation in this world. Amos 9:3 is another reference, as is also Psalm 74:12-15 (note also Isa. 51:9-10). In later Jewish exegesis the dragon is, of course, identified with Satan. Perhaps the most dramatic use of this type of language for God's future destruction of all powers of evil in the earth is found in Revelation 20:2-3; 21:1. In Revelation 21:1 it is stated that when the first heaven and earth have passed away and a new heaven and earth are made, the sea—that is, the old symbol of the chaos of earth—is to be no more: God has conquered evil.

In verses 2-6 the theme of the vineyard of the Lord is used in a sense opposite to its use in 5:1-7. In the days to come God will be the protector of his vineyard; and in verse 6 it is made clear that the vineyard stands for his people.

Verses 7-11 do not seem to be unified, and the connection between the parts is not easy to discern. The over-all theme, however, seems to be an explanation of the suffering meted out to the people by God: it was for the purpose of expiating the guilt and removing the sins of the people of Jacob (vs. 9). Verses 10-11 seem to refer to a desolated city, whether to Samaria or to Jerusalem is not stated. Whichever it is, its people were without discernment and therefore had no favor with God.

In the final section (vss. 12-13), however, there is a remarkable picture of the future time when the people of Israel, scattered now among the nations, will be brought back to the Promised Land and to their common worship of the Lord at Jerusalem. It is this religious dimension in its relation to salvation that has always given Jerusalem a special symbolic power for both Christians and Jews.

THE COVENANT WITH DEATH
Isaiah 28:1—31:9

At chapter 28 the student arrives at prophecies which definitely come from the latter part of Isaiah's prophetic ministry. Chapters 28-31 have their over-all setting in the period between 705 and 701 B.C., when, after the death of the Assyrian emperor, Sargon II, Hezekiah of Judah became the leader of a coalition in revolt against the Assyrians. Apparently what led the king to believe that his action could have a favorable result was his treaty with Egypt in which the latter promised assistance. What

Hezekiah had refused to do in an earlier revolt, between 714
and 711 B.C., he now did. Isaiah was bitter in his denunciation
of this action. Not only was Egypt not dependable (31:1-3), but
it was the height of folly to enter into any treaty designed to
avoid what God had purposed. Consequently, the treaty was indeed "a covenant with death" (28:15). Nothing could come of it
but disaster (28:22; 29:1-10; 31:1-3). The rulers of Judah, an
irresponsible group, mocked the prophet (28:7-14) and tried to
corrupt him and his followers (30:10). In spite of his warnings
the revolt went on, and as a witness against the rebellious people,
Isaiah wrote down what the Lord had told him to say.

"The Bed Is Too Short" (28:1-29)

Chapter 28 can be divided into three sections. The first (vss.
1-13) appears to be a prophecy uttered in the early days of
Isaiah's prophetic ministry against Ephraim (Israel). It is here
repeated in a later context as applied also to Judah in the period
of 705-701 B.C. The prophecy is interrupted in verses 5-6 by a
brief passage concerned with the glorious future beyond the present era of trouble—a feature which is characteristic of the editorial work in Isaiah throughout the book. The prophecy as a
whole is directed against the ruling parties, who are characterized
as drunken and therefore completely irresponsible (vss. 1-4).
Verses 7-8 continue the picture of irresponsible leadership, as-
serting that the religious leaders also are so drunk that they cannot give any accurate word from the Lord. In verses 9-10 the
same leaders of society and government are represented as talking about Isaiah's counsel as though he were a schoolteacher in-
structing children. Verse 10 is not completely clear, although it
seems to be a mocking reference to the procedures of a teacher
with a class. In verse 13 the prophet turns the mocking words
back upon the leaders in a prediction of their fall.

The next section of the chapter (vss. 14-22) deals directly
with the Egyptian covenant. In verses 16-17 the prophet gives
God's word declaring what he has been doing in Jerusalem and
what he intends to do. It is because of God's activity, then, that
the "covenant with death" is to be annulled (vs. 18). Verse 20 is
an eloquent statement of the situation in Judah: "The bed is too
short" and "the covering too narrow"; no one can sleep or keep
warm on this kind of bed. The mention of Perazim and Gibeon

in verse 21 appears to refer to victories of David over the
Philistines (II Sam. 5:20, see margin; I Chron. 14:16).

The final section (vss. 23-29) uses the figure of a farmer at
work in his field, emphasizing the God-given wisdom of the way
in which a farmer carries on his work. The whole appears to be
a kind of parable of the way God deals with people, but it is
exceptional in that one must infer its lesson because no interpretation is included.

Jerusalem Besieged and Delivered (29:1-8)

This prophecy concerning Ariel, a special name for Jerusalem,
is composed of two parts. The first (vss. 1-4) dates from the
period 705-701 B.C. and refers to the coming destruction of
Jerusalem. God's siege against it is compared to David's siege
against the city mentioned in II Samuel 5:6-7. This was a lament,
beginning with the Hebrew word which is translated in 28:1;
29:15; 30:1; and 31:1 as "woe" (see comment on 5:8-23). In
verse 3 we should probably read with the Greek translation "and
I will encamp against you like David." The reason for the use
of "Ariel" for the name of Jerusalem is not known. In verse 2,
however, there is a play on the word, which has the meaning
"altar hearth." That is, Jerusalem shall be like the top of the
altar where burnt offerings are made.

Verses 5-8 portray God's sudden visitation against the foreign
armies attacking Jerusalem, so that the city is saved. This, then,
is a revision of the previous prophecy in the light of the unfold-
ing circumstances which reveal to the prophet God's will. It can
perhaps be interpreted along with 37:21-36 as belonging to a
later Assyrian siege of Jerusalem, about 690 B.C. (see Introduction).

The Present Conspiracy and the Future Salvation (29:9-24)

The remainder of chapter 29 is by no means unified but is
composed of fragments. Verses 9-16 come from the prophecies
uttered in connection with Jerusalem's rebellion against Assyria
in the period 705-701 B.C. The irresponsible action of the government has made the people as insensitive as though they were
in a stupor; they become blind or drunk, so that they can hear

nothing and see nothing (vss. 9-10). Verses 11-12 appear to be
an editorial comment to the effect that the prophet's words are
like a book that is sealed and which no one can read. Men's
minds are regarded as tightly closed and impervious to all sug-
gestions from the Lord or his prophet.

Verses 13-14 refer to the superficiality of the people's religion.
Their worship is a worship of words only, and reverence ("fear
of me") is merely something formal, lacking completely in depth.
Yet God has not finished with his people. He will again do
marvelous things with them, but only after the false "wisdom" of
their supposedly wise has perished. One should note the quotation of verse 13 in Matthew 15:8-9 and Mark 7:6-7, and the
Apostle Paul's effective use of verse 14 as seen in I Corinthians
1:19.

Verses 15-16 refer directly to the conspirators planning the
Assyrian revolt. They are people who pay no attention to the
Lord or, rather, who think that they can hide what they are
doing.

In verses 17-24 there is a sudden change to the distant future
beyond the current darkness. This future will be the time of
restoration and of renewal and of hallowing. The suggestion
that these verses may derive from the period of Second Isaiah is
given support by the reference to Abraham in verse 22. Reference to the first of the patriarchs is very rare in the prophets
and appears elsewhere in the Isaiah literature only in 63:16.

Egypt as "Rahab Who Sits Still" (30:1-17)

Chapter 30, like chapter 29, is organized into two main sections. The first (vss. 1-17) has to do with the "rebellious people"
in the revolt against Assyria, whereas the remainder of the
chapter presents the opposite picture of God as Savior beyond
the time of present trouble.

Verses 1-7 are another ironic lament over the rebellious people
of Jerusalem who have made a league with Egypt without asking
for the counsel of God. Once again Egypt is a people that can
bring no profit. In verses 6-7 there is a reference to the caravans
crossing the dangerous Sinai desert from Palestine to Egypt,
with a reminder of Egypt's "worthless and empty" help. The
name "Rahab who sits still," given to Egypt in verse 7, is as
amusing as it is ironical. Rahab is another name for Canaanite

"Leviathan," the mythological dragon of chaos, the symbol of the unruly forces of nature, and particularly of the turbulence of the ocean. For such a dragon to be motionless is the height of incongruity. Yet that is precisely what Egypt is, and consequently it proves to be a very weak power on which to rely.

In verses 8-17 the prophet is again told to write down his message so that it may be a witness for the time to come (see also 8:16-18). The people are a rebellious lot, and how such people respond to their prophets receives one of its classic biblical statements in verses 10-11. We who have set our own course in history want to hear no word of the Lord that would thwart it, and we make trouble for any prophet who insists that we listen to the word of the Lord in its true form.

In the time of this running back and forth between Palestine and Egypt, what God really wants of Israel is presented in one of the great summaries of all Scripture (vs. 15): The salvation and strength of Israel lie in her repentance, quietness, and trust in God. The people will not have it that way, and for this reason they are in trouble and can expect more trouble.

"This Is the Way, Walk in It" (30:18-33)

In the second part of chapter 30 the editors of the prophecy present the other side of the picture. God does not wish to punish for the sake of punishing. He is waiting to be gracious (vs. 18). Indeed, in verses 20-21 the meaning of the present affliction is beautifully stated: God is a teacher in adversity, but he will not forever hide himself. A final prose prophecy in verses 29-33 would appear to refer to the destruction of the Assyrian army also mentioned in 37:36. If so, then it may date with the very latest prophecies in Isaiah, about 690 B.C.

"The Egyptians Are Men, and Not God" (31:1-9)

Chapter 31, like chapters 29 and 30, is composed of two sections which say opposite things. Here the first (vss. 1-3) is an ironic lament over the Judean government and its supporters, who are relying on the horses and chariots of Egypt and not upon God. Verse 3 so well expressed the problem that it has become one of the best-known verses in the Book of Isaiah.

The second section of the chapter (vss. 4-9) refers to the

salvation of Jerusalem and the destruction of the Assyrian army. Like 30:29-33 and 37:21-36, it probably derives from the very end of Isaiah's life when, in a second campaign of Sennacherib, the Assyrian army met disaster (see Introduction).

"THE LORD IS OUR KING; HE WILL SAVE US"
Isaiah 32:1—35:10

Chapters 32-35 are chiefly prophecies of hope and comfort which are appended to the main body of material collected around the prophecies of First Isaiah. Chapters 32 and 33 probably preserve at least a core of original prophecies by First Isaiah. Chapters 34-35, however, have long been referred by interpreters to the era of Second Isaiah, in the second part of the sixth century B.C.

The Effect of Righteousness (32:1-20)

The first eight verses of chapter 32 picture the state of affairs in society when there is good government, ruling in righteousness and justice. In verse 1 the parallelism between "king" and "princes" seems to suggest that we are to think of God's provision of good government in the future. Then it will be that eyes will see and ears will hear (vs. 3; compare 29:9-10), whereas the folly of the foolish will be curbed. Note the penetrating insight of verse 8: "He who is noble devises noble things, and by noble things he stands."

The second part of the chapter (vss. 9-14) is a prophecy against the complacent women who dance in the harvest festivals and who do not take seriously the coming distress. The prophecy is probably from the early period of Isaiah's prophetic ministry and may be compared to his words against the court ladies of Jerusalem (3:16—4:1). The older prophecy is reused in this place, however, and there have been added to it verses 15-20, which describe the future situation in the new age in contrast with that of the present. In the age to come, God will pour out his Spirit upon all (compare Joel 2:28-29), the barren places of nature will become fruitful, justice will prevail in society, and the result will be peace, quietness, and trust forever. That is, the age of security and righteousness, the time for which all men dream, is indeed one that can be held before our eyes in hope, but its issues lie in God and not in ourselves. Verses 19-20 are unclear in their present context and seem to have been misplaced.

"Your Eyes Will See the King" (33:1-24)

The oracles of Isaiah have been arranged by the editors of the material in such a way that prophecies of judgment frequently are interrupted by either prophecies or hymnic pieces that look beyond the current historical period to God's gracious and marvelous intention of salvation in the future. Chapters 29, 30, and 32 contain alternating materials of this type, as though they were planned to be read in services of worship wherein the prophecies of judgment would be used as occasions for repentance, which would then be followed by the statement of the promises of God. Chapter 33 has similarly disparate material, with verses being set alongside one another in a fairly disjointed fashion so that again we must assume that the arrangement may have been purposive for use in public worship. Verse 1 is a lament addressed to an unnamed destroyer and reminds one of 10:5-11. This is immediately followed in verses 2-4 with a prayer of the people for God to be gracious because they are in trouble. Then verses 5-6 make the positive declaration about God's beneficent intentions.

In the next section, verses 7-9 also refer to a current historical situation in which there is a cry for help; verses 10-16 represent the Lord's answer. Finally, in the third portion (vss. 17-24) the future situation of peace in Jerusalem is pictured, with the Messianic king present. None of the inhabitants will be sick, and all the people will be forgiven for their sins (vs. 24). The climax is the picture of the peaceful Jerusalem in verse 20 and the public acclamation indicating the reason for this happy state: "For the LORD is our judge, the LORD is our ruler, the LORD is our king; he will save us" (vs. 22). Verse 23 is an isolated fragment, the context of which is not preserved.

The Day of the Lord's Justice (34:1-17)

Chapters 34 and 35 belong together in the same alternation of judgment and salvation which is so prominent in the preceding chapters. It has long been agreed by most interpreters that the actual material is drawn from the same circles who have preserved for us chapters 40-66. In verses 5, 6, and 9 the object of God's terrible punishment is spoken of as the country of Edom, which recalls the experience of Judeans when their country was being laid waste by the Babylonians in the period 598-587 B.C. During the weakness of Judah, the Edomites moved into the southern part of the country, annexed it to themselves, and settled it. The prophecy of Obadiah makes further reference to this situation, which becomes the occasion for the prophet's announcement of the Day of the Lord against all nations and all peoples who are in enmity against him. All are called to listen to the Lord's indictment and purpose (vs. 1).

Verse 8 states the prophet's meaning most clearly, "For the LORD has a day of vengeance." The English word "vengeance" no longer translates the meaning of the underlying Hebrew word. "Vengeance" in modern English has only a negative connotation; it refers only to the unjust attitude of a person determined to get even with someone else for some action against him. The Hebrew word, however, is set squarely in the context of justice. It refers to the action of God toward people whose cases have been tried in God's court. The Hebrew word refers, then, to God's carrying out his sentence. Most often it involves vindication, in which case the word should be translated "salvation" (for example, in 35:4 and 61:2). Indeed, long before biblical days it was used frequently with just this meaning. On the other hand, when people are guilty before God, the word can mean his punishing action—and that is what it means in verse 8.

The terror and the bloodiness of the description in this chapter easily repel the reader and cause him on occasion to think that God could not be like this. Yet we must consider the issues of good and evil, justice and injustice, God's struggle for the good and for salvation over against all the forces of darkness and evil which oppose him. We must take these seriously, for otherwise we cannot interpret our history in terms of the providence of God. Indeed, if God's justice is not punishing as well as saving, then man can have little hope, for there will be nothing to stay the forces of evil in history. History is filled with human struggle and with human blood, and the Hebrew prophet faces it frankly and sees working within it the providence of God.

The Highway of the Lord (35:1-10)

This beautiful and triumphant poem could have been written only by one who was absolutely certain of the righteousness of God in history. The whole of nature is represented as being joyful because it will actually see "the glory of the LORD" (vss. 1-2). Then the prophet addresses the weak and feeble, saying, "Be strong, fear not," because God is on his way to save them. Note that the word "vengeance" (vs. 4) in this case again does not render the Hebrew; it can here only mean the salvation of God (see comment on 34:1-17). Verses 5-7 point to the effects of God's coming. The blind, the deaf, the lame, and the dumb all will be healed; and all the infertile places of nature will become fruitful. Then finally in verses 8-10 we hear of the highway from the nations which God will make for the "ransomed of the LORD" to return with joy and gladness to the Promised Land. Note how the last words reach the longing of every human heart: "and sorrow and sighing shall flee away." For the setting of this triumphant and joyful expression the reader should turn to chapters 40-66.

ISAIAH AND KING HEZEKIAH

Isaiah 36:1—39:8

These chapters are a historical appendix to the collected materials in the first part of the Book of Isaiah taken largely word for word from II Kings 18:13, 17—20:19. If, in order to account for the different prophecies of Isaiah concerning Jerusalem, we accept the hypothesis that there may have been two campaigns of the Assyrian emperor Sennacherib against Jerusalem, the first in 701 B.C. and the second some years later, about 690 B.C. (see Introduction), then chapters 36-37 would come from the second of these two periods. Chapters 38 and 39, however, would come from the earlier period, unless chapter 39 comes from a still earlier time, between 714 and 711 B.C., when Babylon had revolted from Assyria and there was a general attempt to persuade many nations to revolt against Assyria (see Introduction).

The Surrender of Jerusalem to Assyria Demanded
(36:1-22)

The editor of the narratives in chapters 36-37 has dated them by quoting II Kings 18:13, "in the fourteenth year of King Hezekiah." This must be 701 B.C.; that is, the year of Sennacherib's campaign against Jerusalem. The curious thing about the Isaiah version of these events is that II Kings 18:14-16, which describes Hezekiah's surrender to Sennacherib and his payment of heavy tribute to save the city of Jerusalem, is omitted. The historical reliability of these omitted verses, however, is confirmed by the Assyrian monarch's own detailed account of the incident. He tells us that Hezekiah was involved in a revolt which included certain cities of the Philistine plain. One of them, Ekron, had a king by the name of Padi who refused to rebel, whereupon he was taken prisoner to Jerusalem and another man was put upon the throne of the city-state. Sennacherib first led his army down the coast, demanded and secured the release of Padi from Hezekiah, and put him back on the throne of Ekron. He then defeated an Egyptian army which had come to help the coalition in a battle of the Plain of Eltekeh, not far from Ekron, following which he turned against Judah. On reliefs found in his palace at Nineveh he portrays his army besieging the Judean frontier fortress of Lachish and himself sitting on the throne receiving obeisance from the leaders of the Judean city. He says that he laid siege to forty-six Judean walled cities and forts, not counting "the countless small villages," and drove out from them 200,150 people, a figure which may well represent the approximate population of Judah at that time. Finally, he says, he made Hezekiah "a prisoner in Jerusalem, his royal residence, like a bird in a cage." The city was besieged but was spared when Hezekiah surrendered and paid the heavy tribute demanded of him.

The account in Isaiah 36:2—37:38 is taken from II Kings 18:17—19:37 and contains a number of very significant differences from the situation in 701 B.C., though the general over-all resemblance of the two is such that one could see how an editor might think of them as one and the same event. This section concerns the miraculous deliverance of Jerusalem from the threats of the Assyrian conqueror. The deliverance was caused by the destruction of the Assyrian army (37:36). That such a destruction occurred during one of Sennacherib's attempts to conquer Egypt appears to be confirmed by the Greek historian Herodotus, who in his history says that the Assyrian army marched across the Sinai desert to Pelusium and there prepared to engage the Egyptian army. Herodotus reports: "As the two armies lay there opposite one another, there came in the night a multitude of field-mice, which devoured all of the quivers and bow-strings of the enemy, and ate the thongs by which they managed their shields. Next morning, they commenced their fight, and great multitudes fell as they had no arms with which to defend themselves." It is possible to interpret this tradition as also involving bubonic plague, which is carried by vermin. In that case the report in Isaiah 37:36 would be in line with it.

An additional difficulty is furnished in 37:9, which indicates that the Ethiopian, Tirhakah, was the king who led the Egyptian army into Palestine to oppose the Assyrians. According to recent information, Tirhakah became king only in 690 B.C., at which time he was twenty years old. This would mean that in 701 B.C. he would have been only nine years old, scarcely of sufficient age to lead an army. Another factor to take into account is the fact that in 701 B.C., Jerusalem was spared and as far as we know very few people were exiled from the country. In 36:17, however, the official of Sennacherib threatens the deportation of all of the inhabitants of Jerusalem. It was Assyrian policy, as a rule, to give a country a second chance for loyalty before destroying it and exiling large sections of its population. The threat in 36:17, therefore, would most naturally be interpreted as referring to a second campaign rather than to the campaign of 701 B.C.

These various points have not in themselves been entirely convincing to all historians. The mention of Tirhakah in 37:9, for example, could be a simple anachronism, while the material in chapters 36 and 37 as a whole would be considered as a popular and less accurate report of the events in 701 B.C., parallel to II Kings 18:13-16. Yet, when the two types of prophecy in First Isaiah in relation to the city of Jerusalem are considered (see Introduction), the assumption of two campaigns of Sennacherib against Jerusalem, one in 701 B.C. and the other between about 690 and 688 B.C., becomes the hypothesis which best explains the otherwise conflicting data.

The narrative in chapter 36 concerns Sennacherib's demand that Jerusalem surrender. He has sent his Rabshakeh from his camp at Lachish as his envoy to Hezekiah in Jerusalem. "Rabshakeh" is not a proper name, but the title of a high Assyrian civilian official. According to II Kings 18:17 he was accompanied by other high military and civilian officials. The place where the officials of Hezekiah met the Assyrian officials was the same as the one where Isaiah had met King Ahaz at another critical moment, over thirty years before (see comment on 7:3). Among Hezekiah's officials at the consultation is Eliakim, who now has the position Isaiah earlier had predicted he would have (22:15-24). That was the office of prime minister of the realm, which we now know to be the signification of the phrase "over the household." The second official was Shebna, called the scribe or "secretary," a position perhaps roughly corresponding to Secretary of State. The third official was Joah, called "the recorder," though a better translation of the Hebrew term would be "herald." That is, he was the officer in charge of all public contacts between the king and the people, perhaps only roughly comparable to a press secretary.

The message which the Rabshakeh has for Hezekiah is very clever and almost unanswerable propaganda. He makes five main points, all asked in a series of rhetorical questions: Do you think words are a substitute for military power and strategy? Do you think you can rely on that broken reed, Egypt? Do you say that you rely on "the LORD" your God? If so, how can you worship him or get an oracle from him when Hezekiah has removed all of the high places and altars so that it is possible to worship only at the one altar in Jerusalem? (This is a very clever reference to the great reform movement which Hezekiah had conducted, and which is described most fully in II Chronicles 29:3—31:21.) Do you have enough remaining military power to repulse a single Assyrian company? Finally, do you think I would come against your country without the support of your God? Indeed, he has said to me, "Go up against this land, and destroy it." (This also was a clever reference to earlier prophecies of Isaiah which interpreted the Assyrian army as God's agent in the punishment of his people; see 10:5-11.)

The colloquy is represented as going on in a public place with a number of people listening. The Rabshakeh's words are so effective that the Judean officials ask him to speak in Aramaic rather than in Hebrew! (vs. 11). At this point the Rabshakeh addressed in a loud voice everyone within hearing (vss. 13-20). He told them that they should not be deceived by Hezekiah, their king. It would be better to make peace with the king of Assyria before it was too late. Has the God of Hezekiah or the gods of any of the nations saved a given land from the Assyrian king's power? In verse 19 and again in 37:12-13, cities are mentioned which the Assyrians had conquered in their push into the west all the way to the border of Egypt in the years since Tiglath-pileser III had come to the throne in 745 B.C. The Assyrian's words were so powerful and frightening that the hearers went in to see the king with their clothes rent as a sign of mourning (vs. 22).

Responses of Hezekiah and Isaiah (37:1-38)

Isaiah's Intercessory Prayer Requested (37:1-7)

Chapter 37 includes several pieces of information of great interest, which were the sequel to the challenge of Sennacherib's Rabshakeh. In the first section of the chapter Hezekiah is said to have put on mourning and to have gone to the Temple for prayer, at the same time sending a commission to Isaiah informing him of what had happened and asking for his intercessory prayer. Isaiah's word for Hezekiah is one from the Lord himself to the effect that Hezekiah should not be afraid. God will deal with Sennacherib; he will hear a rumor and have to return to his own land, where he will be murdered. Whether some report of a palace revolt against Sennacherib actually reached the monarch so that he had to hasten home is unknown. We do know that he was murdered in 682 B.C., some five years after the death of Hezekiah.

Intervention of Egypt and New Message from Sennacherib (37:8-20)

This section involves a second message of Sennacherib to Hezekiah when the Ethiopian king of Egypt, Tirhakah, has led an army into Palestine to oppose the Assyrians. To meet this threat Sennacherib presumably has to break off his siege of the Judean frontier fortresses, but when he does so he sends a new warning to Hezekiah not to let his hopes rise, for no one has ever escaped the Assyrian power.

The warning was contained in a letter which Hezekiah took with him into the Temple. His prayer there is reported in verses 16-20. The reference to God's being "enthroned above the cherubim" is based on the symbolism of the Holy of Holies in the Temple. These two large winged sphinxes ("cherubim") were considered to be the support for God's invisible throne above them (I Kings 6:23-28). Cherub thrones—that is, chairs, the sides and legs of which were fashioned in the form of winged sphinxes —were in common use among the kings of the coastland of Syria and Palestine. The cherubim thus symbolized God as enthroned in sovereignty over Israel and the world. In deep sincerity Hezekiah confesses in his prayer that though it is true that the Assyrians have laid waste nation after nation and cast their gods into the fire, it was because they were simply idols which could be destroyed. The Lord of Israel, however, is "the living God," and Hezekiah prays that God will save Judah so that mankind may know that he alone is the Lord. The divine title, "the living God," seems to be used only when some special emphasis is desired, or when a special point is being made of the active, sovereign nature of the Lord of Israel over against the impotence of the gods of the peoples of the world. It does not mean that God is living as opposed to other gods not living. Instead it means that God is the Creator and Sustainer of life; that is, the Hebrew word for "living" or "life" stands in a predicate relation with "God" in the phrase.

Isaiah's Message for Hezekiah (37:21-35)

A message from the Lord to Hezekiah through the mediation of the prophet Isaiah is now presented. Verses 22-29 form a poetic denunciation of Assyria. In verse 22 Jerusalem is pictured as a young girl making fun of the great conqueror. Then there is a direct address to the Assyrian king and nation from the Lord (vss. 23-29), comparable in some respects with the prophecy in 10:5-19. In verses 23-25 the arrogance and boasting of the Assyrian is depicted. It is as though he thinks of himself as God, whereas he is actually only carrying out what God has planned for him to do (vss. 26-27). All of this braggadocio is actually a defiant raging against God himself. For that reason the king will be defeated and sent back along the road to his own country.

Putting the hook in the nose or a bit in the mouth (vs. 29) is a reference to the Assyrian as to an animal mastered and controlled.

Verses 30-35 are two prose fragments, the first of which (vss. 30-32) promises that there will be a remnant surviving the disasters, one preserved by the Lord. The sign is that by the third year Judeans will be reaping and planting as though nothing had happened. The second fragment (vss. 33-35) is an additional statement concerning God's determination to save and protect Jerusalem against the Assyrian king.

Destruction of Assyrian Power (37:36-38)

Verse 36 recounts the salvation of Jerusalem which is accomplished by the destruction of the Assyrian army. That this was done by "the angel of the LORD" is very likely a theological interpretation of a plague which killed off large numbers of soldiers. This in turn may well be correlated with the information which we have about such a plague in the history of Herodotus. Sennacherib's murder at the hands of his sons took place in 682 B.C. The name of the god worshiped by Sennacherib, Nisroch (vs. 38), cannot be identified with certainty. The spelling is probably corrupt.

The Critical Illness of Hezekiah (38:1-22)

Verses 1-8 and 21-22 of this chapter are a slightly abbreviated version of II Kings 20:1-11. In verses 9-20 there is inserted a psalm of thanksgiving for recovery from illness, the authorship of which tradition had credited to Hezekiah. This psalm is not included in the account in Second Kings.

The narrative concerns an illness of Hezekiah, the nature of which we do not know, though verse 21 seems to suggest that it was a bad boil or abscess, for which a poultice of figs was used at Isaiah's direction. The illness was so severe, however, that the word of the Lord to Isaiah for Hezekiah was to the effect that the king was not going to recover. After a prayer on Hezekiah's part, a second word of the Lord came to Isaiah declaring that God had heard his prayer and would add fifteen additional years to his life. Verse 6 adds the promise that the city of Jerusalem would be delivered from the hand of the Assyrian king. It would suggest that the illness was in connection with the second campaign of Sennacherib against Jerusalem in the period between

690 and 688 B.C. Fifteen years before 690 B.C. would bring us back to 705 B.C., the time when Hezekiah began the plans for revolt against Assyria during the first year of the reign of Sennacherib. Whether the number "fifteen" here is to be taken with that much precision is uncertain. It was probably a round number preserved in the tradition, and it is better to assume that the actual incident of Hezekiah's sickness cannot be dated exactly.

Accompanying the prayer and the promise of additional years to the king's life is the tradition of a sign given by God to Hezekiah in verses 7-8. This is given in somewhat more detail in II Kings 20:8-11. The sign has to do with the shadow cast by the sun on something that is translated "the dial of Ahaz." The reference, however, is to some architectural feature connected with the royal palace in Jerusalem, perhaps an upper story built by King Ahaz, to which one obtained access by climbing a series of steps. The sign has to do with the sun drawing a lengthening shadow on the steps as it declined in the afternoon. In any event, it is quite clear that "dial" is not a proper translation of the architectural feature in question.

The psalm in verses 10-20 is a composition that was probably written for use in a Temple service when a worshiper, after recovery from serious illness or rescue from some dangerous situation, went to the Temple to present an offering of thanksgiving. The Psalter has a number of compositions composed for similar use (for example, Pss. 6, 56-61; see also Jonah 2:2-9). The psalmist begins by lamenting the threat of untimely death, when he will be consigned to the underworld, where he will be separated from "the land of the living" and thus will not be able to see the activity of God. The death of an individual, when it was an untimely death, was a problem to Israelite faith because of the conception of Sheol which Israel shared with her environment. In Sheol everything is the opposite to what it is in life on earth. It is a dark and silent place without activity. Consequently, the real problem of death for the Israelite was that it separated him from the living God and his purposes and activity in history. In the postexilic and Intertestament periods this conception gave way among certain of the Jewish groups to the conception of God's conquest of death and a belief in the resurrection from the dead (Dan. 12:2).

The psalmist continues with a description of his present plight by a variety of metaphors. He has called on God for help until he is "weary with looking upward." All his sleep has fled. In verses 16-19 he prays for deliverance and restoration to health, to the end that in this life he may praise and give thanks to God for his faithfulness. The final verse expresses the certainty that the Lord indeed will save him and that it will be possible to sing songs in the courts of the Temple during the rest of his life.

Verse 22 is evidently a misplaced fragment. In it Hezekiah asks about the sign; and for that question verses 7-8 give the answer as indicated in the fuller form of the narrative in II Kings 20:8-11.

Babylonian Envoys in Jerusalem (39:1-8)

The narrative about the envoys from the king of Babylon is taken from II Kings 20:12-19. If the editor of the material is correct in connecting the visit of the Babylonian ambassadors with the sickness of Hezekiah, then it is probable that the date should be taken as coming very soon after 705 B.C., before Sennacherib had consolidated his position on the throne of Assyria and had assumed firm control over Babylon. The king in question was Merodach-baladan (in its Mesopotamian form it was *Marduk-apal-iddin,* meaning "Marduk has given a son"). He first was able to make himself king of Babylon early in the reign of Sargon II, and he remained in power there from 721 until 710 B.C. When Sargon wrested Babylon from him he fled to his tribal realm in the lower marshlands of Babylonia. In the early years of Sennacherib, when the latter was busy consolidating his hold on the throne, Merodach-baladan again seized the throne in Babylon, but he was able to hold it only a short time before Sennacherib established his own government over the city.

In the biblical narrative the extent of Merodach-baladan's diplomacy in the years 705-703 B.C. is given further support. Under the pretext of Hezekiah's sickness he has sent ambassadors to Judah, presumably to encourage revolt throughout the Assyrian empire. The narrative was probably preserved because of the relation of the prophet Isaiah to the event. The prophet suspected an intrigue and appeared before King Hezekiah to challenge him about the matter. It may be recalled that this was the period of Hezekiah's leadership of the small nations of southwestern Asia in their revolt against Assyria with the backing of Egypt. During that time Isaiah was bitterly opposed to the policies of the king, as indicated in chapters 28-31. Since the Lord, the Sovereign of the universe, is the God of Israel, there is no need to enter into a whole range of political alliances. This was not Israel's purpose in the world, and such alliances were condemned by Isaiah throughout his life. The words of Isaiah to Hezekiah (vss. 5-7) are an anticipation of what actually happened in the fall of Jerusalem to the Babylonians, as described in II Kings 24:10—25:17, over a century later. Whether the words of the prophet are here precisely recorded, or whether the memory of them has been colored by subsequent events, is something we do not know. In any event, verse 8 represents the king as accepting Isaiah's message, because he thought within himself that at least the catastrophe was not going to happen in his own day.

INTRODUCTION
ISAIAH 40-66

As noted in the Introduction to Isaiah 1-39, the historical situation presupposed in chapters 40-55 is that of the middle of the sixth century B.C. Jerusalem lay in ruins (44:26); the Persian king Cyrus was the great figure on the horizon of world politics (44:28; 45:1); Babylon had been the dominant world power but was now about to fall (ch. 47); and the captive people of Israel were shortly to be released from exile by Cyrus and permitted to return to Palestine (45:13). These indicators point to a date about 540 B.C. as the time when these prophecies were composed. A prophet was God's messenger whose duty it was to deliver a message to Israel. The conditions presupposed give us this particular prophet's date. The message in this instance is that "the Lord GOD comes with might" (40:10) to set his captive people free and lead them back to their former homes.

The Assyrian empire weakened and fell in the last quarter of the seventh century. Nineveh, its capital, was destroyed by the Medes and the Babylonians in 612 B.C. The Babylonians (now called also the "Chaldeans") rapidly took over the Assyrian empire, destroying Jerusalem and Judah in 587 (or 586) B.C. for the conspiracy and rebellion which had been encouraged by the promise of Egyptian help. With the death of Nebuchadnezzar, Babylon's greatest king, in 561 B.C., however, this empire in its turn rapidly weakened. Meanwhile the Persian king, Cyrus, united Media and Persia (modern Iran) and then moved into Armenia and Asia Minor, defeating Croesus, king of Lydia, in 546 B.C. In 539 B.C., Cyrus defeated the Babylonian army headed by the crown prince Belshazzar (Daniel 7:1; 8:1) and was welcomed into Babylon itself by its people. Among his first acts were decrees permitting subject peoples who had been dislodged from their homes to return to them. The government was to aid in their resettlement. The Hebrew version of the decree for the release of Judeans is given in Ezra 1:2-4; another decree, permitting the rebuilding of the Jerusalem Temple, was subsequently found in the files of the Persian government and is quoted in Ezra 6:3-5.

The rebuilding of the Temple was completed between 520 and

515 B.C. by a governor named Zerubbabel, a descendant of David (Ezra 3; see Matt. 1:12-13), whom the prophets Haggai and Zechariah believed God would designate as his Messiah who would usher in the new era on earth when the Temple was rebuilt (see Haggai 1:1—2:9; 2:20-23). Chapters 56-66 of Isaiah appear to come from this time of the rebuilt Temple (56:5-7; 62:9). Indeed, 66:1-5 suggests that the prophet or his disciples, in the spirit of First Isaiah, derided the false hopes being placed in the new Temple and accused those so intently concerned with it of choosing that in which God was not pleased. In the past it has been customary to think of chapters 56-66 as reflecting not only a different period but also a different author, sometimes designated "Third Isaiah." While it is true that a number of the interests of this material differ from those in chapters 40-55, the difference is surely to be credited to the changed situation to which the prophecies are addressed. Because of its style and breadth of perspective, such a passage as 61:1-11 can most naturally be considered as deriving directly from Second Isaiah. Indeed, all of the prophecies in the final eleven chapters can safely be credited at least to the disciples of Second Isaiah, and dated about 520-500 B.C., though a specific date for the material is difficult to prove.

Second Isaiah's Message

Hebrew prophecy reaches its highest point of lyrical, joyous expression in Second Isaiah. The days of judgment have passed. Israel has gone through the fire; her iniquity is pardoned (40:2). Now God will come as the Good Shepherd and "will feed his flock like a shepherd" (40:11). The prophecies appear to be arranged in a series of poems, some of which may have come in their present arrangement from the prophet himself. It is seldom that we find lengthy compositions preserved in prophecy, but a number can be discerned here, even though the precise beginning and ending of a given composition is not always clear. The chapters do not present an argument that gradually builds in a rational fashion. Instead, the prophecies center around a few central themes which are looked at from a variety of perspectives and referred to again and again.

The first emphasis to be observed in Second Isaiah is one concerned with the power, universality, and sole sovereignty

of God. If the broken and scattered people are to listen to the
prophet and take heed of his words, then faith must be restored
in him who alone can "renew their strength" so that they may
"run and not be weary," and "walk and not faint" (40:31).

Repeatedly this theme is stated, and on occasion the prophet
will suddenly stop and break into a doxology:

> Sing to the LORD a new song,
>   his praise from the end of the earth! (42:10).

> Sing, O heavens, for the LORD has done it;
>   shout, O depths of the earth . . . (44:23).

Of course, the ground of this praise is not simply the fact that
God is powerful. It is rather that God has used his great power
for the sake of righteousness, which in Israel was understood to
be the salvation of the lost, the depressed, the blind, the weak.
Indeed, the love or grace of God was precisely his use of his
unlimited power to reach down into human society to save those
who had no savior.

Closely associated with the emphasis upon the sole sovereignty
of God is the emphasis upon God as the Creator. The meditation on the nature and identity of God in 40:12-31 makes great
use of God's creative relation to nature. Typical of the thought
and relationship of ideas is 42:5-6. Reference to God the Creator
is simply the preface to the proclamation of God as Redeemer.
He who has the power to create is Lord and Savior. The creation
by God is not set forth as a matter for speculation in and for itself alone. It is a means of proclaiming the sole Lordship of God:
it is the first of his mighty acts in history whereby men may see
and know his sovereignty.

What is God's purpose in his present historical activity? It is
none other than the redemption of all mankind. Distant people
in the time to come "will make supplication to you, saying: 'God
is with you only, and there is no other . . .' " (45:14). To all God
gives this invitation:

> "Turn to me and be saved,
>   all the ends of the earth!
>   For I am God, and there is no other.
> By myself I have sworn,
>   from my mouth has gone forth in righteousness

a word that shall not return:
'To me every knee shall bow,
     every tongue shall swear' " (45:22-23).

The universalism and sole sovereignty of God ("I am God, and there is no other") is so stressed in this prophecy that a previous generation of interpreters believed that Second Isaiah was the first explicit monotheist in the Old Testament. There is no question but that belief in God's use of Cyrus to effect the release of the Hebrew exiles has led the prophet to an unusual emphasis. It is not impossible that he himself lived in Babylon and returned with the exiles, but of this we have no certain knowledge. Furthermore, the desperate need for faith on the part of the broken people led the prophet to a special emphasis on God's sole sovereignty in the world. There is only one God who has been active in history, only one power able to save: "Have you not known? Have you not heard?" (40:28). The prophet's interest is not in elaborating a monotheistic creed; it is rather the upbuilding of faith. But throughout the Old Testament there is such an emphasis upon God as the sole object of religious attention that there is a radical devaluation of all other powers, both divine and human. Hence, the introduction of such a term as "explicit monotheism" into the discussion of Second Isaiah is probably to throw the picture somewhat out of focus.

The Role of God's Servant, Israel

God's agent in his plan of universal salvation is a special people: "You whom I took from the ends of the earth . . . saying to you, 'You are my servant, I have chosen you and not cast you off' " (41:9). The people of Israel as God's servant were blind and deaf; they refused to obey him and he gave them up to "the spoiler" (42:18-25). They have not honored him with worship but have burdened him with their sins (43:22-24). Yet now God is about to do a new thing (43:19; 48:6), and by his prophet he will gird them for their special task.Though punished they have not been forsaken. God repeats his promises to them; they are his chosen ones. Therefore, "fear not, for I am with you, be not dismayed, for I am your God; I will strengthen you . . ." (41:10). He is about to prepare a highway in the wilderness by

which all may return home (40:3; 43:19; compare 35:8-10).
The Persian Cyrus is to set them free (45:13), and though they
once were rebels God now will blot out their transgressions
(43:25). He will pour out his blessing upon them and their descendants, like "water on the thirsty land" (44:3).

The task God expects of them is indeed great. In the current
disorders of the world, Israel is to be witness to all men that the
meaning of all the contemporary situation is to be found only
in the God who has revealed himself and his will in Jerusalem
(43:10-13; 44:1-8; see comment on ch. 41). He alone is Lord;
he alone is in control; his purposes determine the meaning of
history. Israel as God's servant has been given by God as a
"covenant"; that is, as a promise or instrument of salvation, to
give "a light to the nations, to open the eyes that are blind, to
bring out the prisoners from the dungeon" (42:6-7; 49:8-9).
The use of the term "servant" for Israel is fresh and unusual. It
should be borne in mind that the term does not lay the emphasis
on a particularly lowly status before the Lord, but rather on the
service Israel is to perform. The "servant people" are a people
who have a specially given work to do as a service for the Lord.

Four passages in chapters 40-55 have frequently been separated from their contexts and called the "servant poems." They
are 42:1-4; 49:1-6; 50:4-9; 52:13—53:12. While in many other
passages the "servant" is clearly identified as Israel, in these
poems the identification is not made. They read as though an
individual were meant. The sole reference to Israel in 49:3 is
by no means clear. The best-known of the four passages is that
of the "suffering servant" in 52:13—53:12 who "was wounded
for our transgressions . . . bruised for our iniquities; upon him
was the chastisement that made us whole, and with his stripes we
are healed" (53:5). The age-old question about this writing is
that of the Ethiopian eunuch to the evangelist Philip: "About
whom, pray, does the prophet say this, about himself or about
some one else?" (Acts 8:34).

A solution to the difficult problem is made all the more difficult, however, when one begins with the assumption that the
"servant poems" must be severed from their present contexts. It
is often argued today, as in the past, that the servant in the four
passages cannot be separated from the servant in adjoining
passages, who is clearly identified as Israel (for example,
41:8-9; 42:19; 43:10; 44:1). Jewish exegesis has always seen

in the suffering servant of the Lord an interpretation of Israel's past, her suffering in the world, her weakness, her sin, and in the age about to dawn her mission in God's salvation of all people on the earth. The personal vocabulary involves an ancient Semitic manner of thinking and speaking of a group or nation as a single personality. Thus the patriarch Jacob can be pictured as an individual and also as the nation Israel (see, for example, 43:1). A similar phenomenon appears in the New Testament, where Christ can be spoken of as the "head" of the "body" which is the Church (Eph. 5:23), or as the "body" in whom the various members are joined (Eph. 4:12).

In this corporate conception the "servant people" are God's agent in his work of redeeming the world. Second Isaiah sees the whole of God's work with Israel in the past as preparing her for the great mission which is to be hers in the new age that is about to dawn. The royal and the redemptive features of the Messianic theology of Jerusalem have been separated by the prophet in a most original way. God's "anointed," his Messiah, is believed to be Cyrus, whose hand God has grasped "to subdue nations before him" (45:1). God's "servant," however, is one who gave his "back to the smiters," who did not hide his face "from shame and spitting" (50:6), and like a lamb led to the slaughter "so he opened not his mouth" (53:7). Yet God has put his Spirit upon him so that "he will bring forth justice to the nations" (42:1). It will not be until New Testament times that a new and remarkable exegesis of the servant passages will be made. That was to interpret them Messianically, to see them as pointing to the earthly mission of the Messiah. Thus in his life, Christ was the Suffering Servant, but in his death God exalted him, raised him to his "right hand" (Ps. 110) as the royal Messiah foretold of old. It was this new interpretation of Old Testament Messianism that most of the Jews could not accept.

The portrayal of vicarious suffering in chapter 53 is one of the most profound and penetrating conceptions in Scripture. If we allow the prophet some flexibility in his poetic intensity, we can understand the shifting emphasis on the corporate and then on the individual aspects of the servant, until in chapter 53 the latter are used exclusively. The servant, like Moses in the wilderness bearing the burden of his people's sin (see Deut. 1:37; 3:26; 4:21), bears in his body the evil of the world. This vicarious burden led him to be "cut off out of the land of the living"; to pour out his soul to death (53:8, 12). Yet in his giving of himself as an offering for sin the will of the Lord prospers in his hand (53:10). In his willing assumption of the world's burden which leads to death, God's purpose was served —a hard but profound interpretation which throws fresh light into one of the darkest areas of existence.

A New Heavens and a New Earth

Chapters 40-66 of Isaiah are heavily eschatological. That is, the advent of Cyrus on the world scene and the release of the exiles are understood as the beginning of a series of divinely sponsored events which will culminate in the new humanity, the new heavens and the new earth. So confident were the prophets of the goodness of God that they could not believe that the disorder and alienation present in the world are the final meaning of history, or that human sin could finally thwart God's purposes, or that God would fail in the plan expressed and implied in his promises to Israel. Before the destruction of Jerusalem and its Temple in the summer of 587 B.C. (or 586), the prophets saw that coming destruction as the first stage in the series of eschatological events. First Isaiah interpreted the fall of Israel in 733-721 B.C. in the same way. Second Isaiah lived after the punishment of Israel was over. The next event is restoration and the servant's service as a "covenant," a light, for all men. In this context we read the remarkable invitation to the eschatological feast: "Ho, every one who thirsts, come to the waters . . . Come, buy wine and milk without money and without price. . . . Seek the LORD while he may be found . . . For you shall go out in joy, and be led forth in peace . . ." (ch. 55).

From the time of the rebuilt Temple comes the description of the Temple as "a house of prayer for all peoples," for foreigners and even for eunuchs (56:3-8), whose service in royal courts had forced upon them the bodily change which, by an old law, meant that they, too, were excluded from the innermost courts of worship. Chapters 57-59 have much that reflects the spirit of denunciation of the older prophecy. A restored community is actually in existence, and its life is in contrast to its purpose. Yet in chapters 60-66 the proclamation of the coming God again predominates.

The redemptive service and the nationalistic glorification of Israel, however, are at times not kept in balance in this material. On the one hand, it is said: "You shall be called the priests of the LORD, men shall speak of you as the ministers of our God" (61:6). Yet at the same time it will be claimed that, having been depressed and persecuted for so long, Israel in the new era will be the chief of all peoples and the nations will be Israel's servants. "For the nation and kingdom that will not serve you shall perish" (60:12). "You shall suck the milk of nations" (60:16); "you shall eat the wealth of the nations" (61:6). While, after terrible suffering, the desire for such a radical reversal of a people's fortunes is humanly understandable, it is nevertheless far removed from the picture of the servant role of Israel to be found in chapters 40-55.

Yet through and beyond it all there is deep faith in the salvation of God. "The LORD will be your everlasting light" (60:19-20). His salvation is at hand. His eradication of the world's evil will soon be seen (chs. 59, 63). The Lord comes to judge the whole earth, to purge it, to change it.

The prophetic hope in the New Creation is an expression of faith in the dependability of God. In the New Testament this hope was taken up in the Christian faith as the future which God has promised in the Parousia (the second coming of Christ). It has had a powerful influence on the Western world as one of the Bible's most creative portrayals. As distinct from the religious situation in Far Eastern countries, the Bible has trained the West to think of history as a meaningful procession of events en route to a goal. Even among those who have completely secularized and materialized human goals, as among Marxists, the biblical promise has set meaning within human affairs, and this life has become a meaningful effort. The struggle for humanity is worth the cost because this creation is not in itself evil. Man can hope and work and plan, for the evil that now prevails and defeats man's hope of earth is not eternal.

Of course, there have been Christians in every century who have read the biblical words as though they were a kind of literal prose, a blueprint of the future instead of a poetic and symbolic portrayal of faith and truth that can be proclaimed in

no other way. In every Christian century there have been those
who were sure that the biblical prophecies of the future were
to be literally fulfilled in that very time. All have been wrong.
God's time and man's time are not the same. Both the Church
and the Synagogue have had to learn to await God's time. Yet
these pictures of the future are a vital and integral part of
biblical and Christian faith. By them we can know the direction
of the future; we can shout aloud in faith even in time of
tragedy, for we know that man's sin cannot finally defeat the
Lord of all creation and redemption. This hope and faith are
what can energize the ethical struggle of the present, because
the ultimate future is on the side of those who love and labor
for the welfare of their fellow men.

OUTLINE
ISAIAH 40-66

Introduction to the Prophecy. Isaiah 40:1-31
The Call of the Prophet (40:1-11)
Proclamation of God's Saving Power (40:12-31)

The Plans of God for Israel and the World Revealed. Isaiah 41:1—48:22
The Assembly of the Nations (41:1-29)
The Servant of the Lord (42:1—43:7)
Israel as God's Witness in the Assembly of the Nations (43:8—44:23)
Cyrus and the Salvation of the World (44:24—45:25)
The Fall of Babylon and the Salvation of God (46:1—48:22)

The Mission of Israel. Isaiah 49:1—55:13
The Servant of the Lord Commissioned (49:1-26)
"The Lord God Has Opened My Ear" (50:1-11)
Encouragement of Zion (51:1—52:12)
The Lord's Suffering Servant (52:13—53:12)
"Your Maker Is Your Husband" (54:1-17)
Invitation to the Banquet of the Lord (55:1-13)

Prophecies from the Rebuilt Jerusalem. Isaiah 56:1—66:24
Divine Exhortation (56:1—59:21)
"Arise, Shine; for Your Light Has Come" (60:1—66:24)

COMMENTARY
ISAIAH 40-66

INTRODUCTION TO THE PROPHECY
Isaiah 40:1-31

The Call of the Prophet (40:1-11)

The interpretation of 40:1-11 has been somewhat a matter of debate. The discovery of the complete scroll of the prophecy of Isaiah in Cave 1 at Qumran, however, presents us with a text very much like that of the traditional Hebrew text, but which has in verse 6b, "And I said, 'What shall I cry?' " instead of the reading in the text which was translated in the King James Version, "And he said . . ." This reading focused attention on certain of the ancient versions which have the same reading. It is now accepted, therefore, as in the Revised Standard Version, that the verse is to be interpreted as the prophet's own response to a voice which calls him to prophesy.

The second perspective that has become much clearer through recent study, and that now makes certain the interpretation of this section, concerns the prophetic vision of the heavenly council from which each prophet received his summons to the vocation of announcing the decisions of the heavenly court (see Introduction to Isaiah 1-39 and the comment on ch. 1). Thus in 40:1, God addresses some hearers and commands them to give comfort to "my people." In verse 3 one of those who has been commanded issues a proclamation calling for the preparation of a highway through the desert for the coming God. In verse 6 a second voice gives the prophet his call and continues with the message that he is to proclaim to Israel. There can be no doubt that the voices in verses 3 and 6 are those of messengers or angels from the heavenly court, and it is they who are addressed in verses 1-2. We have here, therefore, the call of the prophet and the announcement of God's new and dramatic intervention in historical affairs for purposes of salvation. The call of Second Isaiah is closely parallel to that of First Isaiah recounted in chapter 6, except that the situation and the content of the prophecy are completely different.

For Second Isaiah, God's message is that the judgment of Israel is past; "her warfare"—that is, her period of draft into military service—is at an end. She has been punished more than enough, and her sin is now pardoned. Now God is going to come as Deliverer! The announcement in verses 3-5, taking the form of a command to prepare a highway for the coming God, is a theme found also in chapter 35, in which verses 8-10 indicate that "the ransomed of the LORD," the people of Israel scattered among the nations, shall walk along that highway through the wilderness back to the Promised Land. The common imagery is that of the journey through the wilderness from Egypt under the direction of Moses. In this event God's "glory"—that is, the revelation of himself in the world—will be revealed, and it will be seen by all mankind (40:5).

In verses 6-11 the message which the prophet is to proclaim is summarized by the heavenly messenger. It speaks of the transitoriness of all things on earth, which are like grass and flowers that quickly wither and fade, and contrasts this with the permanence and stability of the promise of God.

This note is followed by the joyous and triumphant proclamation of the God who now is to come with power and mercy. For beauty, the portrayal of God as the Good Shepherd (vs. 11) is surpassed nowhere in Scripture and is equaled only by Psalm 23. In verse 9 there is some textual uncertainty as to whether the prophet as the herald of good tidings is addressed (see margin). The interpretation that Zion or Jerusalem herself is the herald who is to proclaim the great news to the world is probably the correct one.

Behind the words of this prophetic call one can sense the exultation, the joy, and the triumph in the prophet's mind and voice. The stage is now set for the remarkable portrayal in the following chapters of the meaning of the events of current history and the proclamation of the great eschatological program of God.

Proclamation of God's Saving Power (40:12-31)

The remaining part of chapter 40 is not in the form of prophecy, but is rather the prophet's discussion and proclamation of the creative power of God. The reason this is placed before the prophecy proper which begins in chapter 41 is to be inferred

from verse 27. The people of Israel have been broken, their
cities have been destroyed and their leading groups scattered
in exile. They are thus dispirited and can be expected to give
little response to any prophecy until or unless a lively faith is
restored. The prophet hears them saying, "My way is hid from
the LORD, and my right is disregarded by my God." It is as
though God had cast them aside and forgotten them. To
counter such a lack of faith the composition in this section was
drafted. It deals with 'the everlasting God, the Creator of the
ends of the earth," who alone can give "power to the faint" and
"to him who has no might . . . increases strength" (vss. 28-29).

The first section, in verses 12-17, draws attention to God as
the Creator, who is directed by no one, who needs to consult
with no one, who does not need to be taught by anyone. He is
complete in himself, and is of such majesty, power, and great-
ness that "the nations are like a drop from a bucket" before
him (vs. 15). All of those who are mighty in their own eyes
on earth are very small indeed in the total perspective of God.

This then raises the question in verses 18-20 as to how one
can properly talk about such a Deity. Both in these verses and
again in verses 25-26 the prophet makes clear that there is
nothing in the whole range of heaven and earth that can be
said to be like God. No human categories of thought or of
language can possibly depict him as he is in himself. God's
eternal being is something completely hidden from man. It is
his own mystery, and he has given no one the ability to penetrate
that mystery. Our minds are too small to have any comprehen-
sion whatever of what God is really like as he is in himself.
That is the basic mystery of time, of space, and of human
existence. Consequently, those who engage in the ordinary
religiosity of earth generally manufacture their own gods to
suit their taste. Thus, in verses 19-20 the prophet pours scorn
on those who manufacture for themselves idols. To the typical
Hebrew the great religions of the ancient world were simply
idolatry, the worship of man-made fetishes.

In verses 21-24 and in verses 27-31 the prophet answers his
own problem. Has it not been revealed to Israel from the beginning that the true God is he who is enthroned as Sovereign,
not inside his creation but outside it? The creation is like a
tent stretched over a space in which people may live. He who
created this world is one before whom its inhabitants are very

small indeed and its great rulers as nothing. The reference here, as in Genesis 1, is to the Hebrew understanding of the world. It was not a world like our own, with cosmic space filled with galaxies of stars and their planets. Instead, heaven was a semi-circular globe resting over the earth and keeping out the waters of the great deep, so that man and all living things might have a free place in which to multiply and live in generation after generation. The fresh and salt water rivers and oceans on the earth were connected with their sources in the great deep beyond. The sun and moon, the planets and stars, were lights which God had hung in the firmament of the sky to furnish light by day and by night and to set the times and the seasons by which men could measure and divide their days and years (Gen. 1:6-19). However, while this to us seems to be a very limited universe, people in subsequent ages have found in the picture a symbolic expression that can be a conveyer of profound religious truths to those living with a very different understanding of the universe. The basic point remains valid even in our time: what God is in himself is beyond all our human knowing because we are too small and he is too great. Yet all that exists is in complete dependence upon him. The whole heavenly host is his creation, and he has made and named them all (vss. 25-26).

At this point the prophet then asks Israel in effect: How is it possible for you to believe that such a God as this has disregarded you? Have you not been taught from of old that this God "does not faint or grow weary, his understanding is unsearchable"? (vs. 28). This, then, is the God who actually possesses the power to raise up the fainthearted and the exhausted. Those who place their hope and their confidence in this God may "run and not be weary, they shall walk and not faint" (vs. 31). This God has the power to do what he wants. If he says that he will do a thing, he can be relied upon to do it. He alone is worthy of deep respect, faith, and devotion. Those who give it will never be disregarded or cast away.

THE PLANS OF GOD FOR ISRAEL AND THE WORLD REVEALED

Isaiah 41:1—48:22

The Assembly of the Nations (41:1-29)

Chapter 41 constitutes the first major prophetic poem in Second Isaiah. Some interpreters would include 42:1-4 within the bounds of the poem, but it is better to include the first of the so-called "servant poems" in the next poem, all of which has to do with God's servant.

God is represented in chapter 41 as speaking in the first person, calling for an assembly of all the nations to decide on the meaning of the current history. This scene draws in a very original way upon the picture of God and the divine council of which in pre-exilic times the prophet was thought to be the herald. Yet in this case the judgment scene is pictured as taking place on earth among all the peoples of the earth, and the issue to be decided is whether or not God—and he alone—is the Lord of history. It forms a most powerful bit of comparative religion, the gods of the peoples of the world being shown to have no power or directing control over human history.

The Summons and the Subject to Be Discussed (41:1-4)

The prophecy begins in verse 1, in a summons to all the nations of the world to come together "for judgment"; that is, to decide on an issue. The use of the term "coastlands" and similar words in Second Isaiah is to be taken as designating all peoples of the world. Phoenician advance through the Mediterranean and even into the Atlantic Ocean has furnished for this prophet a large horizon. He is conscious of the larger world beyond the immediate axis of the Nile and the Euphrates.

The issue to be discussed is described in verses 2-4. The figure of the Persian conqueror Cyrus is now dominating the horizon. Nation after nation falls before him. Why is this possible? What does it mean? The answer is given in verse 4. It is the Lord who has made himself known to Israel who alone is responsible for these world-wide and earth-shaking events. Thus, though the answer to the question is stated at the outset, God wishes this fact to be acknowledged by all men. Moreover, the impotence and foolishness of human idolatry is to be shown for what it is. Note the way the question is phrased. It is the characteristic Israelite question: What is the meaning of history? Human events have running through them a purpose, one that needs to be searched out before it can be discerned.

The Nations Prepare Their Idols (41:5-7)

After the introduction in verse 1 and the first strophe in verses 2-4, the second strophe in verses 5-7 represents the peoples of the earth as in fear and turmoil over the current events. They are working frantically to prepare their gods who are expected to give answer in the great assembly concerning just what is going on in the world and what it means. Instead of providing a tolerant, penetrating discussion of the theology of polytheism, the prophet with scorn and biting sarcasm considers the whole thing a man-made effort. He sees human religiosity on this earth as meaningless and stupid. These handmade gods are all that the people have for the interpretation of human history and destiny!

God Prepares Israel as His Witness (41:8-20)

With the third strophe (vss. 8-10) attention shifts to Israel, who is to be God's witness in the great assembly of the nations. Israel is the one who will testify as to the true meaning of events, because to her alone has the secret been revealed. First, however, this witness must be prepared for her task. As a broken people, she must be strengthened and have her faith restored. In verses 8 and 9 the story of Israel's life is interpreted as having been the work of God. Those who were no-people (see Hosea 1:9) were collected from the ends of the earth; they were chosen by God to be his servant. This reiteration of the old promises is meant to affirm to the exiled people that they are still God's servant, that he has indeed chosen them and has not cast them off.

Israel is addressed directly by God, and her identity is given as the family of the patriarch Jacob, "the offspring of Abraham." The nation is spoken of further as though she were a single person: "Israel, my servant." Here is the first appearance of a term that is central to Second Isaiah and is original with him. This term is "servant." It refers not primarily to a particularly lowly status before God in the world, but instead to the service which Israel has been called to perform. The servant of the Lord is

God's appointed officer; the term, in fact, carries with it considerable dignity. Israel has an extremely important status in the world. She has been called to special service by the great King of the universe.

In verse 10, God's address to Israel through the prophet strikes now at the very center of the people's current problem. They are neither to fear nor be dismayed, for the Lord declares: "I am with you . . . I am your God; I will strengthen you, I will help you, I will uphold you." God never calls a servant to a task without empowering him to do it. He is constantly present with his servant. Faith and not fear must be the servant's response, for otherwise the service will not be performed as God wills it to be. The words in their original context addressed a broken and dispirited Israel. At a later time they will be seen as applicable also to the Church as God's servant people in the world.

The thought of verse 10 is now continued in the fourth strophe (vss. 11-13). Israel no longer needs to worry about her enemies. They shall disappear, because "I, the LORD your God, hold your right hand; it is I who say to you, 'Fear not, I will help you.'" Israel, God's Covenant people, hears God's strong reiteration of the tie between them. Their greatest enemy is fear. God has called them to their task and he will stand beside them in their performance of it. The faith called for now is the faith which can move mountains.

In the fifth strophe (vss. 14-16), the exhortation not to fear is repeated in still another context. God will make Israel strong, strong enough to be an instrument of divine judgment in the world, a threshing sledge with sharp teeth. Instead of fear, Israel is to have joy in the Lord, to rejoice and to glorify "the Holy One of Israel." Here, then, there appears one of First Isaiah's favorite titles for God, one that characterizes the whole Isaiah literature. In verse 14 the phrase "worm Jacob" strikes our modern ear as somewhat peculiar. The term means something that is small or few in number, and it is clearly meant as a term of endearment.

In the sixth strophe (vss. 17-20), God's direct address to Israel having ended, there appears a short hymn which describes the way God works in the world and his providence which surrounds those with eyes to see it. The poor and needy in a desperate plight in a parched desert, as Israel had been long ago in the days of Moses, are the object of God's saving action. He will transform the desert into a marvelous, well-watered

garden, so that all men everywhere may know and identify
God as the One who has done it. This hymn draws on old
themes to reassert the fact that the whole work of God with
Israel in the past and in the future is for the sake of the whole
world, that all may know that he and he alone is God.

The Challenge to the Gods of the Nations (41:21-29)

It is presumed that the assembly of the nations has convened
(vss. 21-24). Now God challenges the gods of mankind to set
forth their case, to interpret the past and what is to happen.
The verbs in verse 22 probably refer to the various rites of
divination by which ancient people sought to find out about
the future. God challenges them to use all of their ancient arts
that man may know the meaning of the historical events. In
verse 23 the statement is ironic. The gods are asked to do something, either good or bad, so that people may know they are
gods and that man may be brought to awe and reverence and
respect before them. We may assume that in the presentation of
the prophecy there was a pause for purposes of suspense. The
gods give no answer: they are dumb and silent. Then in scorn
God says: "Behold, you are nothing, and your work is nought;
an abomination is he who chooses you" (vs. 24).

Here the gods of mankind are attacked at their weakest point.
None of them were ever devised as lords of history. The Bible,
uniquely among the religious literatures of the world, proclaims
a God who is not only the Lord and Creator of the universe but
also the Sovereign of human history, continuously at work within
it to save man from self-destruction.

The last strophe (vss. 25-29) contains God's affirmations concerning his own work in history. There is no one in the whole
world who has been able to state the meaning of the advent of
Cyrus on the scene of human history. God is the first and the only
one who has revealed the meaning of current events. He declared
it in Jerusalem by his herald, the prophet. The gods of the nations
are a delusion; they are simply nothing, "empty wind."

The Servant of the Lord (42:1—43:7)

The paragraphs in chapter 42 and 43:1-7 all have to do
with Israel as God's servant, with the exception of two (42:
10-17). The whole section may be viewed as a unified composi-

tion, though we cannot be completely certain whether it was put together in its final form by Second Isaiah himself or by his disciples who preserved and transmitted the prophet's words. In the first section (42:1-4) God through his prophet introduces or presents his servant and describes his mission to the world. Next (vss. 5-9) God addresses his servant and explains what the servant's mission is to be. The section ends in verse 9 with the triumphant assertion that the old order is at an end; the new is at hand, but before it comes to pass God will tell his servant about the coming events. At this point a hymn of praise is introduced (vss. 10-13). Since it does not seem to have been quoted from another source but appears to be the composition of Second Isaiah himself, there is every reason to believe that the hymn was placed purposely at the point where the announcement of the "new things" is made. In verses 14-17 it is as though the thought in verse 9 were continued. God describes his purposes of redemption in the current history. In 42:18-25 the past actions of God in relation to his servant are expounded and defended. The servant has been the blind one, and God was led to punish him, though he did not take the punishment to heart. Finally (43:1-7), God's redemption of Israel is described as the new Exodus, a new passing through the waters. The exiled of Israel will come from the north and the south and from the ends of the earth.

God Introduces His Servant (42:1-4)

This is the first of what many interpreters have called the "servant poems." The servant is spoken of in the third person and his mission is described. When one sees the number of times that the term "servant" is used throughout these chapters, however, it becomes a very subjective judgment which holds these verses to be separate from their context and perhaps by a different author. If they are treated in the context of the assembly of the nations (ch. 41), and if the concentration is on Israel as God's servant to whom the secrets of history are revealed (42:9) and who are to be his "witnesses" in the assembly of the nations (43:10), then we may interpret the poems as God's formal presentation of his servant to the peoples of the world.

God's special relation to the servant is described in verse 1. The servant is the chosen one on whom God's favor rests. Filled with God's Spirit, his task will be to bring forth God's saving justice to all mankind. The "Spirit" of the Lord in the Bible is that agency which God sends to work within individuals to the end that they may be empowered to do the work he would have them do. The term "spirit," meaning "breath" or "wind," thus is a metaphorical term, representing God as "breathing into" people, "inspiring" them to do his work. It is a very successful way of speaking about God's active though always mysterious work among people.

In carrying out his mission as the mediator of the righteousness of God to the nations, the servant is to be an agent of peace and of nonviolence. He will not make any noise; he will not even break a reed already bent. Nevertheless he will faithfully bring forth justice. The time may be long, but the servant will continue his mission until the new order is accomplished. The term "justice," used in synonymous parallelism with "law" in verse 4, is in Second Isaiah identical with the righteousness of God; that is, God's reaching down in human affairs in order to save those who are lost. The servant, in ways which are not specified, is to be the mediator of this justice or this saving action to the world of men. As befits its nature, the work will be done quietly, patiently, and without violence.

God Commissions His Servant (42:5-9)

The prophet now hears God address the servant directly. Yet the introductory statement about God in verse 5 speaks of him as the Creator. All that is has its source in him. It is he who has called Israel and given her a mission to the nations. The themes of creation and redemption are held together as one and the same. God the Creator is the sovereign Lord of all; his purpose is to save the world. For that purpose Israel is chosen.

Verses 6 and 7 give a remarkable statement of God's work in Israel and the purpose of it. God first introduces himself: "I am the LORD, I have called you in righteousness." The mission of Israel as a servant is to be "a covenant to the people, a light to the nations, to open the eyes that are blind, to bring out the prisoners from the dungeon . . ." The phrase "covenant to the people" has been much commented upon, and its meaning is not entirely clear. In the context, however, it clearly refers to a saving activity of God, of which Israel is the agent. The term "covenant" is parallel to "a light to the nations." Since "covenant" refers to a way God has of relating himself to people, we presumably are to interpret the prophet's meaning somewhat as follows: Israel is to be God's mediator to the world, God's agent who proclaims to the world the identity of the God who would draw all men into relationship with himself. This is the nations' light and hope. This is their deliverance from the prison in which they now sit.

The final two verses of this section (vss. 8-9) refer again to God's determination to be God and God alone, with no rivals among the idols of mankind. This is the God who is now about to bring forth new things which he will reveal to his servant before they come to pass.

A New Song: Hymnic Interlude (42:10-13)

With God's announcement of the "new things" the prophet now pauses to introduce a hymn of praise. The whole world and all that is in it is called upon to give praise and glory to the Lord. Verse 13 is written in the style of Israel's early war poetry (for example, Exod. 15:3; Deut. 32:39-43; Judges 5:4-5). God's dramatic action in the present scene is compared to that of a great warrior, a fighter of battles who acts "zealously" (the meaning of the term translated "fury"), who shouts aloud the battle cry. This use of warlike language to describe God's activity in the world is a dramatic portrayal of his effective power and his determination to carry out his plans without defeat.

God Explains His Purposes (42:14-17)

Verse 14 contains a metaphor unusual as applied to God. For a long time he has held his peace, until now he cannot restrain himself. Like a woman in childbirth he cries out, for his plans and his purposes can be held back no longer. The world-wide turmoil is the action of God. The world of nature will be transformed. The blind will be led by a path they do not know. This is what God has determined to do. Those who turn to their idols and say, "You are our gods," when they are completely powerless to do anything, will be utterly put to shame (vs. 17).

God's Past Treatment of the Servant Expounded (42:18-25)

The mention of the "blind" (vs. 16) now leads to a discussion of the past history of God's servant or messenger, who has indeed been blind and deaf. God having spoken his indictment through his prophet (vss. 18-20), the prophet now continues the exposition in his own words, referring to God in the third person. For his purposes of salvation God chose to make his 'law" (the teaching or doctrine about him) great and glorious, but Israel could not see or understand what God meant. So they have become a people "robbed and plundered," the prey of the nations. Who did all this to Israel? "Was it not the LORD, against whom we have sinned, in whose ways they would not walk, and whose law they would not obey?" (vs. 24). God punished his servant, but the servant was so blind and deaf that he still did not understand what was going on.

This section is cast in the style of the older prophecy. It asserts the truth of what the former prophets had said: namely, that Israel had been destroyed for her sin of rebellion. What the prophet here laments is that Israel appears to have learned so little from her history. Nevertheless, as the next section goes on to explain, God has indeed chosen her. (In 43:22-28 the theme of the past history is again introduced, but here, though Israel has indeed sinned and sinned repeatedly, God declares his forgiveness and his blotting out of her past evil.)

God's Redemption of Israel (43:1-7)

The prophet now turns from the past to the future, and proclaims in more detail the theme he began in 41:8-10. The great scenes of old are reiterated and used to expound the coming redemption of Israel; that is, God will bring the exiles forth from among the nations so that the people of Israel will be reconstituted. In verse 1 note the verbs, "created," "formed," "redeemed," and "called." All are used in clauses that are put together in parallelism with one another and build up to the thought at the end of the verse, "You belong to me!" Though Israel has been broken and scattered, God's work of old still holds true. Israel is his people. The word here for "create" is the same as that used in Genesis 1:1. It is generally used in the context of a special creative activity of God; here it is applied to the formation of a special people. The word "redeemed" has a special background in Hebrew. It is a term that arises out of the legal background of family law. At the death of a member of the family it is the responsibility of the next of kin to "redeem" the deceased's property so that it does not pass from the control of the clan, and it is also his duty to "redeem" the deceased's widow by marrying her, taking care of her, and seeing to it that a family is raised up for the man who has died. This term is now applied to God's action in forming the nation: saving them from Egyptian slavery and giving them the Promised Land. They have a special family relation to him. He is active in relation to them as a next of kin, and he has given them a name. They who were no-people are indeed a people, and they are God's.

The prophet continues with allusions to the past, which he generalizes and uses to interpret all of God's actions in the past and in the future (vss. 2-4). God will be with them in whatever they have to do, even though it be a new crossing of the sea (Exod. 14-15). In verse 3 the picture of the negotiations necessary for the freeing of the enslaved evidently has as its background the story of the Exodus, but in the foreground is the coming conquest of Egypt by the Persians (under Cambyses in 525 B.C.). God did this as a "ransom," and it was a heavy price which he had to pay. He was willing to do it, however, "Because you are precious in my eyes, and honored, and I love you" (vs. 4). The manner of speech here is highly metaphorical, and it seems not possible to give it a precise historical interpretation. In the strongest possible way the prophet sees God affirming his love for Israel, the broken people, and stating his willingness to pay any price, even the highest of ransom payments, for her salvation.

The exhortation, "Fear not," is repeated again and again in Second Isaiah as in verses 1 and 5. God is with his people. They need not fear. He will bring them from the four corners of the earth, every one of them who is designated as a member of God's people whom he created for his "glory"; that is, for the revelation and honoring of his name in the world.

Israel as God's Witness in the Assembly of the Nations (43:8—44:23)

The prophet's proclamation now returns to the assembly of nations (43:8-9), and then to Israel, God's witness, and the message she is to proclaim before the world (43:10-13). This leads to a repeated proclamation that God is going to do a new thing: he has prepared a second Exodus of his people (43:14-21). That is, as soon as Second Isaiah introduces the theme of Israel's mission among the world of nations, he turns immediately to the question of God's salvation in order that the faith of the broken community can be restored. As background, verses 22-28 speak again of the past when Israel "burdened" God with her iniquities. That is the reason he delivered her to destruction (vs. 28). This is followed in 44:1-5 with the description of the New Israel formed by God's Spirit. In 44:6-8 the prophet turns to the message which God wants Israel to proclaim. In the whole of the past there has been only one effective power and force in the world, and that is God himself and none other. This leads to a long insertion which in transmission has lost much of its lyric character: 44:9-20 is a satirical essay on the man-made idols of the human race. Then the prophet hears God's appeal to Israel to return to him, after which there is a triumphant call to the whole assembly of heaven and all the peoples of the earth to break forth into singing (44:21-23).

The Nations Assembled (43:8-9)

The trial scene of the nations, first introduced in 41:1-4, is again introduced. The blind and deaf nations of the world are called to assemble. The issue to be decided is the meaning of the current history and the past preparation for it. The peoples of the world are challenged to bring forth their witnesses who can give testimony that will be acknowledged as correct.

Israel's Calling as God's Witness (43:10-13)

The mention of witnesses in verse 9 is followed by God's direct statement to Israel: "You are my witnesses." What Israel is to know, believe, and understand, and what she is supposed to proclaim to the world, is that the God who has declared himself to Israel and made himself known in his acts of salvation is God and God alone. There is no savior apart from him. "I am God, and also henceforth I am He; there is none who can deliver from my hand; I work and who can hinder it?" (vs. 13). In the midst of a world full of gods, this dramatic and forthright clearing out of the vast amount of underbrush is remarkable testimony. The focus of religious attention must be single. In the whole action of God in the past, as he has made himself known to Israel, there has been no other power associated with him. He alone has done it, and of this fact Israel is to be the witness before the world. His is the only effective power in the world. What he chooses to do none can hinder.

God's New Salvation Reiterated (43:14-21)

No sooner has this forthright message been given to Israel as the sum of her testimony to the world, than the prophet immediately turns back to the theme of Israel's coming salvation. God is going to send to Babylon and break down the bars of her prison and lead a new Exodus. The concentration in verses 18-19 on the new things which God is about to bring forth as over against "the former things" should not be interpreted as though the former things were without meaning for the present. It is, instead, a matter of getting the servant of the Lord to look forward to a future which the nation assumed it did not have. A highway is to be prepared in the terrible desert, and God himself will lead his people across it. They need fear no wild animals, nor will they go without water. God will do this for the people he has formed for himself "that they might declare my praise."

Here are gathered together in one short poem many of the themes of the prophet with regard to Israel. There is a strong and insistent emphasis upon Israel as God's chosen people. His acts in the days of old in forming a nation for himself were not in vain; they were not annulled in the Assyrian and Babylonian destructions of Samaria and Jerusalem. Now is the time of the new Exodus, the New Israel. This is the "new thing" which will be far more glorious than the first Exodus. Central in the prophet's words, however, is the purpose of God's action: it is that Israel shall be his witness before the world.

God's Past Indictment and Judgment of Israel (43:22-28)

The prophet now turns abruptly from the present and future to the past sin of Israel, reiterating the correctness of the messages of the earlier prophets. Israel has not been burdened with a heavy sacrificial system, and as a result her people have not had to bring many offerings of various types. Yet at the same time they have not brought God worship at all but have burdened him with their sins (vss. 22-24). In verses 26-28 God challenges Israel to present her case in court and let the matter be equitably decided. Every one of Israel's leaders or mediators has sinned against God, and that is the reason why Israel was delivered to "utter destruction." The term so translated is an old word drawn from the institution of holy war in Israel's early days as a nation, when pagan peoples and property were to be offered up as a holocaust to God. This was a way of purifying the land, and of hallowing it for the new use to which it was to be put. The prophet proclaimed that God was using Assyria and Babylonia to bring holy war against Israel, and here the reference is to the destruction of the nation as a purifying holocaust. Nevertheless, always in the background is the statement that the punishment is past and that God has blotted out the nation's transgressions (vs. 25).

The New Israel by God's Spirit (44:1-5)

The prophet hears God's voice reaffirming to Israel that she is his servant, his chosen, and saying again, "Fear not." The thought in verses 3-5 now turns to the new nation of Israel that is to be formed. God will pour out his Spirit and his blessing upon her future offspring so that they will be as numerous as grass and reeds by a flowing stream.

Israel believed that during the first period in the Promised Land, the period of the Judges, God ruled Israel directly and for periods of crisis raised up leaders and empowered them by his Spirit to do their work. In prophetic eschatology God's new age will be a time when the New Israel will all be possessors of the Spirit. The most familiar statement of this work of God among the future people is Joel 2:28-29. In the New Testament this prophecy of the age to come is seen as having been fulfilled in Christ. The Church is nourished and formed by God's Spirit, and her birthday is at Pentecost, when the disciples experienced the outpouring of God's Spirit in their midst (Acts 2).

Israel's Message as God's Witness (44:6-8)

The message to which Israel is to be witness before the world, first specified in 43:10-13, is now described again. There is no other effective power in the universe than the God who is Israel's Redeemer, "the LORD of hosts." If there is, let that power speak up and explain the past and the future. Yet, the people of Israel need not be afraid; God's sole sovereignty had been revealed to them of old and they are his witness. There is no other "Rock" on which they can rely. This is the first use in Second Isaiah of one of the old words used to describe the dependability, the strength, and the protection of God. God as the "Rock" is a sure and strong refuge and protection in time of danger. (See, for example, Deuteronomy 32:4, 15, 18, 30, 31; I Samuel 2:2; and II Samuel 22:2-3 for earlier and very effective uses of the same metaphor, which is also common in the Psalms.)

Satire on Idols and Their Worshipers (44:9-20)

The original text of Second Isaiah seems to have been interrupted at this point for the introduction of verses 9-20. Verses
21-23 could well be interpreted as a proper continuation of
verses 6-8. The original poetic structure of verses 9-20, if there
was such a thing, is no longer clear. Yet even if the verses owe
their present expansion to the school of Second Isaiah, the
spirit of the great prophet himself and some of his characteristic
phrases are present. As a response to the question and its answer
in verses 7-8 this section on idolatry is a remarkable satire. People who make their own gods and set them up as witnesses are
in a pitiable situation. Such witnesses "neither see nor know,
that they may be put to shame" (vs. 9). After a detailed description of the making of an ancient image (vss. 12-17) and of
the way a human idol-maker uses part of the same wood to burn in
a fire to cook his food and to warm himself, the prophet or his
disciples portray the plight of the idolater with the greatest possible irony by remarking, "He prays to it and says, 'Deliver me,
for thou art my god!' " (vs. 17). People who do this sort of
thing simply have no discernment whatever. They do not ask,
"Shall I fall down before a block of wood?" Such a person "feeds
on ashes; a deluded mind has led him astray, and he cannot deliver himself" (vss. 18-20).

Of course, no polytheist of antiquity would have acknowledged these words of the prophet as a fair description of his
religion. The ancient idols were in no way meant to confine the
great cosmic deities. They called the great gods to the mind of
the worshiper and, since they were "like" the gods they stood
for, they in some measure shared in the divine holiness and
could be used as proper foci of attention in worship. The
Israelite prophet, however, refused to acknowledge that there
was any reality whatsoever behind the image. To him the ancient
worshiper was trying to worship a fetish, something that had no
power to do anything. We see the prophets to have been correct in
this adverse judgment, because it is true that the religions about
which they were speaking died with the death of the people and
civilizations which had formulated them. The ancient gods died
when their civilizations died!

"Remember These Things, O Jacob" (44:21-23)

The precise object of the term "remember" in this section

is unclear. In the present editing of the text of the prophet it would refer to the section on idolatry and the sole Lordship of God (vss. 6-20). Yet verse 22 seems to refer back to 43:22-28. God has forgiven all of their earlier transgressions and now invites his people: "Return to me, for I have redeemed you."

At this remarkable announcement of the graciousness of God, the prophet suddenly calls for the whole host of heaven and all that is on earth to break forth into singing (vs. 23). The great deed of God has been decided upon and can be spoken of as having been completed: "For the LORD has redeemed Jacob, and will be glorified in Israel." The joy and the triumph of this prophetic faith and of its vision of God's future is one of the significant characteristics of this literature.

Cyrus and the Salvation of the World (44:24—45:25)

The Sovereign Purpose of God (44:24-28)

This passage is unusual in its form. After an introduction, "Thus says the LORD, your Redeemer, who formed you from the womb" (vs. 24a), the prophet quotes God's identification of himself as the Lord, and this is followed by a long series of participial phrases (in Hebrew) which in English are rendered by relative clauses. First God identifies himself as the sole Creator of the heavens and the earth (vs. 24). He is one who frustrates the work of the diviners and magicians of the world, the whole vast realm of the occult art which filled the life of ancient man. In contrast, he fulfills "the word of his servant" and "the counsel of his messengers." The latter reference is to his people Israel in their capacity as God's servant and messenger in the world (chs. 41-43). Israel is interpreted here, however, as God's prophet, with God's word to be announced and proclaimed. The background of this passage would appear to be Deuteronomy 18, where Israel is told that she can have nothing whatsoever to do with all the occult arts of magic, divination, astrology, or spiritualism; instead, when God wants her to know something he will send his prophet, one of her own brethren, who will speak plainly so that all can understand. Here Israel is seen as fulfilling this office for the whole world.

In verses 26b-28 the references become more specific. Jerusalem is uninhabited and the cities of Judah are in ruins, but God promises that they will be rebuilt. He who promises this is the

one who can control the great watery deep (vs. 27) which surrounds the world. Finally, the rebuilding of Jerusalem and of the
Temple in that city is to follow the work of the great Persian
conqueror, Cyrus, who is God's shepherd (vs. 28). The term
"shepherd" here refers to an important officer or administrator.

Cyrus, God's Anointed (45:1-8)

The name of Cyrus having been introduced in 44:28, the
prophet now turns to this great figure and explains explicitly that
he is the Lord's "anointed." Up to this time the special term
"anointed"—meaning anointed by the Lord—was used generally
for two offices in Israel, that of the priest and that of the king,
both of whom were anointed with holy oil (Lev. 21:10; I Sam.
10:1; 16:1, 13). The title was especially used, however, as the
theological name of the Davidic king in Jerusalem. To use the
term as a title for Cyrus means that he is one whom God has
especially appointed to a position of royal responsibility in the
world. In the verses which follow we are informed that God has
commissioned Cyrus to use his power "to subdue nations before
him," to open doors, to cut bars of iron; he will be given access
to the secret places where treasure is hidden among the nations.
That is, at this moment Cyrus is God's king. Here in Second
Isaiah, then, the office of the Messiah appears to have been re-
interpreted. His redemptive functions in the world are assigned to
Israel as God's servant and witness; the use of the needed power
and force to break the resisting and alienated powers of the
world is the task given to Cyrus, the "anointed."

In verses 2-6 God addresses Cyrus directly, giving him a commission. The power of Cyrus is actually the power of God, who
has called him for the sake of his servant Jacob and Israel his
chosen (vs. 4). It is God and God alone, the God who has made
his identity known to Israel, who has called and empowered
Cyrus, even though Cyrus does not know it. The work of Cyrus
is actually another of the great works of the Lord, who creates
both light and darkness, weal and woe. Here the prophet breaks
forth in a hymnic form (vs. 8), calling upon heavens and
earth to bring forth the righteousness which God has created, the
righteousness which is God's power used for the salvation of man.

For the Hebrew prophet nothing goes on in the world that
is not under God's control. The great conquerors of ancient time
are able to do what they are doing only because they form part

of the over-all purpose of God in history (see also 10:5-11). The work of Cyrus was indeed a saving work in the sense that he allowed the oppressed peoples of the Babylonian empire to return to the homes from which they had been exiled, if they wished to do so.

Who Dares Deny God's Sovereignty? (45:9-13)

At this point it is as though the prophet hears someone scoffing at the tremendous assertions being made about the effective power and purpose of the God of Israel. He utters, therefore, a true ironic lament or "woe." The pronouncement of a funeral lament over someone who has done something wrong is used by the prophet as a device for announcing divine judgment. One does not enter into an argument or a contention with his Maker any more than an earthen vessel does with its potter. The clay does not talk back to the one who is fashioning it any more than one challenges parents to explain what they are doing when they bring children into the world. In verses 11-13 the prophet quotes God directly in answer to those who question him, and again he hears God reiterate that he is the Creator of the whole world, of the heavens and the earth and all their host. It is he who has aroused Cyrus, and he "will make straight all his ways." He does so because Cyrus is going to set the exiles of Israel free and rebuild the city of Jerusalem but "not for price or reward." It is indeed true that under Cyrus and Persian rule these precise things happened and a little province of Judah with a rebuilt city of Jerusalem and Temple within it was created. The greatest of the Persian monarchs can be said to have been among history's most enlightened imperialists. The Persian policies and accomplishments would appear to faithful Israelites as the work of their Lord. He alone among the gods of the world is the sole Creator and Determiner of destiny, the Lord of time who has put purpose into human events.

"Turn to Me and Be Saved, All the Ends of the Earth" (45:14-25)

The prophet's vision now turns to all the peoples of the earth and the effect upon them of God's work in Cyrus and in Israel. In verses 20-21 the theme of the assembly of nations appears again (see ch. 41; 43:8-13). Here it is to be noted that the purpose

of this vision of a world assembly is to proclaim to everyone that
God alone is the effective Director of human destiny, whereas
the gods of the nations are nothing but dumb idols. Thus, in
verses 14-17 the nations of the world, having been subdued by
Cyrus, are in complete religious confusion. At the same time
they will see how Israel has been saved by the Lord, and Israel will
not be put to shame for all eternity. Then they will turn to Israel
and bow down to her, saying, "God is with you only, and there is
no other, no god besides him" (vs. 14). Verse 15 is not clear.
The translators interpret it as an interjection of the prophet: Of
a truth God is one who hides himself; that is the reason he has not
been known to the nations. It can also be argued, however, that
the verse is simply a continuation of the concession of the nations:
"Truly, thou art a GOD who hidest thyself, O God of Israel, the
Savior." That is, the God of Israel has made himself known only
in Israel. In this sense he has hidden himself from the world. To
learn of him mankind must come to Israel, who as God's prophet
will proclaim his name and his will.

In verses 22-23 the great invitation to the nations is given:
"Turn to me and be saved . . . By myself I have sworn, from
my mouth has gone forth in righteousness a word that shall not
return: 'To me every knee shall bow, every tongue shall swear.' "
That is, God's word with the purpose of salvation of mankind
has gone out into the world and will not return until it has accomplished its purpose. In the course of time everyone who is
alienated from God will turn to him, because only in him is there
saving righteousness and the power to do what he wills.

In Second Isaiah the missionary role of Israel and God's determination that the whole world shall be his Kingdom is more
clearly and forcefully set forth than in any other part of the
Old Testament. The Christian Church has read these verses as
having been fulfilled in Christ in the mission of the Church. As
a matter of fact, this is still the Christian hope. God has not
finally fulfilled this great vision of universal redemption. Both
Jews and Christians, therefore, share a faith in the God who one
day will remove the world's alienation from him. (For another
hymn which has the same vision, though in another context, see
2:1-4 and compare Micah 4:1-4.)

The Fall of Babylon and the Salvation of God
(46:1—48:22)

Lesson from the Gods of Babylon (46:1-13)

The prophet now expounds in the name of God the lesson that exiled Israel is to take from the fall of Babylon. The chief gods, Bel and Nebo, are idols which have to be carried on beasts when their people try to rescue them from the hands of Cyrus. The greatest of the gods of the Babylonian religion cannot save their country or their people but must themselves go into captivity! Bel is a title meaning "Lord" (Baal in Hebrew) and here refers to Marduk, the head of the pantheon of gods worshiped in Babylon, whose great temple, Etemenanki, was the chief religious edifice in the city (see Jer. 50:2; 51:44). Nebo is the Babylonian god Nabu, who was regarded as the son of Marduk and whose major temple was evidently at Borsippa, another Babylonian city. Behind the imagery in 46:1-2 lies the procession of the gods in the annual New Year's festival in Babylon during April, when the images of Marduk and Nabu were carried in the festival procession.

The prophet now addresses Israel in God's name, seeking to bring home the lesson. God has carried her from her birth, and even before birth, and he will continue to carry her even into her old age (vss. 3-4). The people are again challenged with the question of whether it is even conceivable that the God of Israel should be compared with the idols which can do nothing (vss. 5-7). This leads to another assertion of the sole Lordship of God and of his consistent purpose to carry out what he has planned (vss. 8-11). Israel is called to "remember this and consider, recall it to mind." Therefore the "stubborn of heart" are to listen to the Lord's promise and put their faith in his words: "I will put salvation in Zion, for Israel my glory" (vs. 13).

It will be noted that Second Isaiah returns again and again to this theme. His purpose for a dispirited and faithless people is to stir up faith and trust and willingness to follow. His emphasis is on the power and purpose of God in history. The God of Israel is the Lord of history, and in history are the signs of his active working. Israel is called to remember his works of old.

But now the prophet announces a new action of God. Israel is appealed to again and again from a number of different perspectives to listen to this proclamation, to give it heed, and to give it entire faith.

Address to Babylon (47:1-15)

God now is represented by the prophet as addressing Babylon directly. She is pictured as a young woman who must descend from her throne to sit in the dust and to labor as a menial. The Redeemer of Israel, the Lord of hosts, the Holy One of Israel, is about to "take vengeance" (vss. 3-4). The English word "vengeance" has today only a negative connotation, although at one time it had a positive meaning also, the sense of "vindicate." The Hebrew word so translated is not represented at all by the meaning of the modern English word. It refers to God's just control over the world. In the case of Babylon, the reference is to God's just and judicial decree that she is to be punished and destroyed by the emperor Cyrus. On another occasion the "vengeance" of God may be salvation. Whether it is judgment or salvation depends upon the relation of the recipient to God.

The problem of the great conqueror is expressed in verse 7. Babylon presumed that she was to be mistress of the world forever. For this reason she showed no mercy to those in her charge. She thought that she alone was god ("I am") and there was no one else, but her day is now at hand (vss. 8-9). In her wickedness she presumed that there was no one and no power who could either see what she was doing or do anything about it, but now the judgment of God is upon her.

In verses 12-13 there is a vivid reference to the divination and magic which were such a prominent part of Babylonian life. The people may stand fast in their sorceries and continue the attempt to predict the future by astrology, but none of this has power to save them in the crisis. The destruction is at hand, and "there is no one to save" (vss. 14-15).

Babylon as a world power, like Assyria before her (see Isa. 10:5-19), has had her day, and it is over. Her empire will now be included in an even larger empire, that of the Persians. She has served God's purposes. Now her turn has come to be punished for her self-idolatry and wickedness. (For other

partly contemporary prophecies concerning Babylon in the
Isaiah literature, see especially 13:1—14:21.)

"I Make You Hear New Things" (48:1-22)

The movement of thought in this chapter appears to divide
into three parts. Verses 1-11 return to the subject of "new
things." Verses 12-16 return to the subject of Cyrus and God's
claim to have sent him. Finally, verses 17-21 make a renewed
assertion of the coming release of Israel from exile. Two poetic
lines in this chapter do not seem to be a part of the otherwise
apparent unity. The first is the last line of verse 16: "And now
the Lord GOD has sent me and his Spirit." Elsewhere in the
chapter the prophet is conscious only of quoting God's word
directly; it is strange that suddenly at this point he refers to
himself and to God's Spirit as having been especially sent to
announce the "new things" or, in this particular context, the
arrival of Cyrus on the scene of history. For this reason a
variety of changes have been suggested to make the meaning
fit in with the context, but without solving the problem. Moreover, it is not improbable that the prophet should have explained
his mission as a part of God's present activity.

The other line of poetry that does not seem to be in its
original context is verse 22: " 'There is no peace,' says the
LORD, 'for the wicked.' " Virtually the same line appears also
in 57:21, where it does seem to fit its context. Consequently,
one suggestion has been made that Second Isaiah's editors have
taken the verse from that place and repeated it here as the
conclusion, not simply of chapter 48, but of the whole first
section of the prophecy, extending from chapter 40 to this
place. One would still wonder, however, how appropriate this
verse is as a summary of the prophet's message in this section.
It is again a question for which we have no clear answer.

This chapter, then, is basically a recapitulation of the first
section of the prophecy and of its major themes. In verses 1-11,
with rising crescendo the prophet returns to Israel with words
of exhortation, explanation, and assurance. He wants them to
understand that the former great events that took place in the
creation of Israel as a people in the Promised Land and the
great events in her subsequent history are all the work of God.
Israel has always been an obstinate group (vs. 4), and as a
result God declared these events in advance lest any should say

that someone other than the Lord did them. Having heard and seen all this, they are now to know that new things never heard of before are going to be done. God alone is the Lord of human events. All this has been announced but not really heard, and the people have continued to rebel (vs. 8). Therefore God has tried them as in a furnace and has refined them. He has done this for his own sake; that is, for the sake of his purpose in the world. The prophet is very conscious of the fact that there is no other conception of God in the world like this one. Opposition to the prophets time and again took the form of a denial that God was thus active in history (see 5:18-19; 29:15; Micah 2:6; 3:11; Zeph. 1:12). From that time until this, people have found it easier to change their conception of God than to change their own ways. But this, too, is idolatry; it is what the psalmist means by the statement, "The fool says in his heart, 'There is no God' " (Ps. 14:1).

In verses 12-13 God identifies himself again as the sole Lord and Creator. Then in verse 14 the prophet briefly returns to the theme of the great assembly of the nations in order to announce again that Cyrus, the Persian conqueror, is the Lord's man. It is God's purpose that will be performed on Babylon; Cyrus has been appointed by God, and God will see that his way is prosperous (vs. 16).

Finally, the Lord again turns to Israel as their Redeemer (vss. 17-21). In verses 18 and 19 there is another reference to Israel's past history. If only the nation had listened in previous times they would not be in their present situation. Nevertheless, their release from captivity is at hand: "The LORD has redeemed his servant Jacob!" (vs. 20).

THE MISSION OF ISRAEL
Isaiah 49:1—55:13

The second major section of the prophecy of Second Isaiah is concerned almost completely with Israel as God's servant and with the work that the servant is called upon to perform in the world. The themes of chapters 40-48 are not left entirely aside, but a concern with the mission of Israel will now be especially emphasized. This fact plus the originality, the faith, and the universal perspective of the prophet combine to create the greatest missionary passages in the Old Testament. For that matter, they may be placed alongside the finest missionary passages in the New Testament, where the Christian Church has seen their fulfillment. These particular poems are to be seen in 49:1-13; 52:13—53:12; 55:1-13.

The Servant of the Lord Commissioned (49:1-26)

"I Will Give You as a Light to the Nations" (49:1-13)

Chapter 49 appears to be a poem complete in itself. Like chapters 34 and 41 it begins with the formal summons to the nations to hear, in this case God's commissioning of Israel as his servant. It ends with the great assertion of verse 26: "Then all flesh shall know that I am the LORD your Savior, and your Redeemer, the Mighty One of Jacob."

The first six verses, or according to some interpreters the first seven verses, constitute what has been called "the second servant poem," 42:1-4 being the first. In this case the servant is represented as speaking in the first person, describing to the nations God's call and commission. The problem with regard to interpretation is whether the so-called servant poem is an original composition of Second Isaiah, and thus a vital part of the whole poem of chapter 49, or is to be separated from that context and interpreted by itself alone. In the case of 42:1-4 a separation is to be rejected because the conception of "servant" is such a central and vital part of the prophet's message. When seen in the context of the theme of the great assembly of the nations, Israel as the "servant" is an appointed official to witness before the whole world to the sole sovereignty of God in history and in current events. The passage in 42:1-4, therefore, simply cannot be separated from its context, if one is to make sense of the whole of Second Isaiah's understanding. A similar argument can be advanced in connection with 49:1-6. A special problem exists here, however, that does not exist elsewhere in the servant passages. In verse 3, as in 41:8-9 and 44:1, God identifies his servant as "Israel, in whom . . . [he] will be glorified." God had called the servant even when he was still in the womb of his mother, and has prepared him as a man would prepare a sharp sword or a polished arrow. In verse 4, then, Israel makes a confession that in the past she has spent her strength for "nothing and vanity," but now she acknowledges completely that her "right" and her proper service are in the Lord. At this point, therefore, Servant Israel is represented as accepting her new commission as proclaimed by the prophet in the previous chapters. The problem expressed in 40:27—namely, that Israel felt that her right was disregarded by God—is now solved in this affirmation.

The problem for the interpreter, however, appears in verse 5. In verses 1-4 Israel in response to God's urging has freely acknowledged that the Lord has called and commissioned her to be his servant. Now the thought turns to the task of the servant. The Lord has formed her "from the womb to be his servant, to bring Jacob back to him, and that Israel might be gathered to him" (vs. 5). How can it be the task of Servant Israel to restore Israel as the people of God? Some interpreters have tried to solve the question by deleting the word "Israel" from verse 3. There is, however, little possibility that this can be conceived as the correct solution to the problem. There is no real evidence for such a deletion among the ancient manuscripts, and the word is needed for the rhythm and balance of the poetic line. The most commonly given solution to the problem is to see in the prophet's concentration upon Israel as the servant a focus of attention upon the *true* Israel, that righteous remnant or core of the nation whom the earlier prophets had attempted to call forth out of the people as a whole. There is little question but that in the prophets a wedge is being driven between the nation as a whole and the true Israel who in faith and obedience are the remnant which becomes the real people of God. If this is the correct view, then verse 5 means that the Lord has formed his servant, the true or "ideal" Israel, to restore the whole nation in the Promised Land. Another suggestion is to assume that verse 5 is to be interpreted as follows: The Lord who formed Israel from the womb to be his servant has said that it is now his purpose to bring Jacob back to him. This is defended on the ground that in the earlier chapters God is always represented as Israel's Redeemer. While this interpretation is possible, verse 6 certainly reiterates the view that it is part of the servant's task to restore the nation of Israel.

The world-wide nature of the servant's mission, with the rejection of a purely nationalistic interpretation of that mission, is given remarkable expression in verse 6. It is not a sufficiently important task simply to restore Israel alone. The restoration of Israel as a nation would be without meaning if that event were separated from the purpose for which Israel exists in the world. Here Second Isaiah rises above every nationalistic tendency and is to be placed at the head of the whole prophetic movement. The only purpose for the existence and restoration of Israel is that as a servant she may become "a light to the nations," and that through her service God's salvation may "reach to the end of the earth." The term "light" is, of course, one of the Bible's most remarkable symbols. In the first chapter of Genesis, darkness is considered to be a part of the primordial chaos into which the light came; thus the whole work of God in revelation and redemption in the world can be interpreted as "light." Israel's task among the nations is now that she be a "light," that is, an agent of a divine salvation.

Verse 7 provides the introduction of a theme that will be central in 52:13—53:12. Here Israel, as God's servant, is one who is deeply despised by the nations; she is "the servant of rulers." Yet now God promises that in the great saving events to come, the kings of the world will see and understand the important role which Israel has for the salvation of the world. At that time they will do Israel honor.

The second main part of the poem on the commissioning of the servant appears in verses 8-13. Again, as in 42:6, God through the prophet tells Israel that he has given her as "a covenant to the people"; that is, as the means whereby all the peoples of the world will come into relation to the Lord of the world. Again it is asserted, as in 42:7, that this vocation involves the liberation of prisoners and all those who are in darkness. The reference to "Syene" in verse 12 represents a correction of the Hebrew *Sinim*, which no one has been able to understand. Syene is modern Assuan, at the first cataract of the Nile in Upper Egypt. In verse 13, as in 42:10-13, the prophet interrupts the discourse to exhort the heavens and the earth and all that is in them to sing for joy, for the Lord has comforted and had compassion upon his afflicted people. This suggests that the thought of the prisoners and those in darkness who are to be released (vs. 9) turned the prophet's mind to exiled Israel. Thus we see that the last part of verse 9 and verses 10-12 are to be interpreted as applying to the return of Israel to Jerusalem and the Promised Land (compare 43:1-7).

"I Am the Lord Your Savior" (49:14-26)

The prophet's thought now turns to Zion (Jerusalem) and to the devastated country of Palestine. Zion is represented as saying, "The LORD has forsaken me, my Lord has forgotten me" (vs. 14). The following verses (vss. 15-21) provide God's assurance that the wasted and desolate places are going to be built up. People are now gathering and will shortly be streaming back into the country, until there will be a population problem and children will say, "The place is too narrow for me; make room for me to dwell in" (vs. 20). Zion has been as one "bereaved and barren, exiled and put away" (vs. 21), but now she will be astonished at the vast numbers of those born in exile who will be returning to repopulate the land.

The thought of return from exile is continued in verses 22-23, as God now addresses the exiles directly. The peoples of the world and their rulers, finally understanding the importance of Israel in God's planned salvation of the world, will actually assist the exiles to go back home and will bow down to the ground before them as an evidence of their respect. When that happens, declares God, "you will know that I am the LORD; those who wait for me shall not be put to shame" (vs. 23).

In the final strophe of the poem (vss. 24-26) the release from exile is likened to the capture of prey from a tyrant. Israel is assured that God will contend for her and will save her children. "Then all flesh shall know that I am the LORD your Savior" (vs. 26). It may be remarked that Israel was indeed released from exile, and that those who wished to return home were enabled to do so (see the Books of Ezra and Nehemiah). Yet the full realization of this prophecy did not then come about. The salvation of the world and the mission of the servant of the Lord have been continuous, and for the final accomplishment we still devoutly hope. God's time has proved to be of longer duration than was apparently conceived in the prophecies regarding the future in both the Old and New Testaments. Yet the importance of the prophecies is that they point the direction in which God's work in history is even now moving. Without such directional signals in the chaos of human events it would be impossible to know to what one should commit his life. The eschatological pictures of the prophet thus provide part of the basis for ethical action in the present, while at the same

time they assert in faith that there is indeed a future and that
we are called as the servants of God with a mission in the
preparation of that future.

"The Lord God Has Opened My Ear" (50:1-11)

The unity of this chapter has often been challenged because
its three main parts do not seem to hold together. Verses 4-9
constitute what has been called "the third servant poem"; in
it, as in 49:1-6, the servant speaks in the first person. This
section is preceded in verses 1-3 by a metaphorical reference
to Israel's past experience as a divorced wife. It is followed by
a section (vss. 10-11) in which the words are clear enough,
but how it is that they are to be interpreted is not at all clear.
The three sections of this chapter, then, are somewhat cryptic
in their relation to one another. While various theories have
been posed, none can be said to be anything more than a guess
as to the reason for this situation.

In the first verse there is a reference to Israel as a divorced
wife of the Lord. It is God who is speaking to the children
and asking where the bill of divorce is and to which creditor
the children were sold. (For a similar use of this figure see
Jeremiah 3:1 and Hosea 2:2-13.) The metaphor likens the
Covenant between God and Israel to a marriage (see also ch.
54) and the punishment of Israel to a divorce. The "bill of
divorce" is that document which a husband was required to
give when he declared that the marriage was over (Deut. 24:1-
4). The prophet hears God ask why it is that when he has now
come to save there is no one to reply (vs. 2). Is it because
he has no power? (For the figure of speech about the shortened
hand see also 59:1.) On the contrary, God alone has all power
and can do what he wills. Therefore, the divorce and the selling
of the children are not final or permanent. God is about to
redeem them.

In verses 4-9 Servant Israel responds in the form of a confession. The servant confesses that it is God who has taught
him and who has opened his ear, and he was not rebellious
against the teaching. He did not hide himself from those who
smote him and put him to shame. Instead, he put his whole trust
in the God who helps him and who will vindicate him. The task
which has been put before him (49:5-6) is here accepted by

the servant in the faith that although he is weak he will trust God to give him the strength for what he must do.

In verse 10 the prophet now asks publicly who it is that walks in darkness and yet trusts in the name of the Lord. That is, who now in reverence obeys both the Lord and the voice of his servant who has been commissioned and has accepted the commission? Verse 11 could perhaps be interpreted as a response to that challenge. In any event, those who have no further illumination than the light of their own fire will find it a torment rather than a blessing. While the verse is not clear with regard to its original context, in its present setting it is possible to interpret it as a warning against those with little faith.

Encouragement of Zion (51:1—52:12)

In this section the themes which were begun in 49:14-21 are recapitulated in a rising crescendo of power and beauty. The servant has been called and commissioned, and he has acknowledged and accepted the Lord's hand upon him (50:4-9). Now the prophet addresses those who remain in Jerusalem, a city which is lying in ruins. Note the vigorous verbs used in the exhortation: "Hearken" (51:1,7), "Listen" (51:4), "Awake" (51:9; 52:1), "Rouse yourself" (51:17), "Shake yourself from the dust, arise" (52:2), and the like.

"The Lord Will Comfort Zion" (51:1-16)

In the first seven verses of this prophetic poem God speaks through the prophet to the people who are remaining in the waste places of Zion (Jerusalem). In the first strophe (vss. 1-3) he calls upon them to look to "the quarry" from which they have been digged; that is, to Abraham and to Sarah whom God called and whom he has "made . . . many." It is for a purpose that God did this, and the people who remain in Zion are the heirs of his stated promises to Abraham. Thus Zion should be comforted because the Lord is going to make her like the Garden of Eden. In verses 4-5 there is a reference to God's law and justice going forth as "a light to the peoples," a salvation for all mankind (see Isa. 2:1-4; Micah 4:1-4). When this takes place, the present heavens and earth will vanish (vs. 6). This last reference points forward to the prophecy of the new heavens and the new earth (65:17; 66:22-23).

The coming release of Israel from captivity and the rebuilding of Jerusalem are connected in the prophet's mind with the end of the current age, when God's kingdom will be world-wide in extent and when there will have been a shaking of the foundations of the universe and a reconstruction of heavens and earth. This hope as it continues in the Intertestament period is called "apocalyptic" eschatology; it differs from the eschatology of classical prophecy in the sense that there is increasingly little reference to any concrete historical circumstance on earth. The people of God in the time after the Exile will think of themselves as living in an interim, awaiting these glorious events. In the New Testament the same apocalyptic understanding will continue, being changed only in so far as the new age is to be related to the second coming of Christ. Mark 13 and Matthew 24-25 are particularly vivid illustrations of this hope arising out of the teaching of Jesus. In these passages, however, the theme of Christian watchfulness is introduced as a kind of symbol of the whole ethical life of the Christian, who remains alert, watching for the signs of the coming of the Son of man.

Ethical responsibility in the present was a theme that could be developed as a watchfulness and a service because the direction in which God intended history to move was known. Similarly, Judaism in the postexilic period developed a conception of a constitutional law which described in detail how God wished to be worshiped and served in the interim within the delayed eschatology. That is, the development of classical Judaism was a result of the delay in the complete fulfillment, as over against a partial fulfillment, of such prophecies as this.

In verses 9-11 the prophet speaks in his own name, calling upon God to awake and "put on strength" as in the days of old. The question, "Was it not thou that didst cut Rahab in pieces, that didst pierce the dragon?" is a reference to the Canaanite creation myth in which the dragon which symbolized chaos was variously named as Rahab, Leviathan, Sea, and Serpent. It was thought that Baal slew this dragon at the beginning of time, and that in this act world order was established over against chaos (see also 27:1; Job 41; Ps. 74:12-17; Amos 9:3). The poetic allusions to this myth in the literature of Israel are a way of saying metaphorically that God is the Creator. It is he who vanquished chaos. The defeat of the dragon is connected with the drying-up of the sea so that Israel could get across the

border of Egypt and thus to freedom (vs. 10; see Exod. 14-15).
Creation and the Exodus redemption are here related and are
used as the model for the fulfillment of the promise that "the
ransomed of the LORD shall return, and come to Zion with
singing" (vs. 11).

The final words in the first section are words of comfort
addressed by God directly to the fear which the people have
concerning the future (vss. 12-16). The Lord is the Maker of
Israel, the Creator of the universe, the Protector of his people
against their enemies in the days to come, and he now says to
Zion, "You are my people" (vs. 16).

"Your God Reigns" (51:17—52:12)

Jerusalem is here pictured as one who is staggering with
intoxication, having drunk the cup of the Lord's wrath (vss.
17-23). Yet the Lord informs the people of the city that he
has now taken away this cup and has given it into the hands of
the tormentors of Jerusalem.

This is the setting for the new exhortation to Zion to awake
and put on her "beautiful garments," for she is going to be
set free from captivity to foreign powers (52:1-2). The judgment has passed to those who have enslaved her (vss. 3-6).
As Israel had been sold into slavery to these people without
charge, so they are now to be redeemed without money.

At this point the prophet inserts a hymn (vss. 7-12) which
describes the coming of God to Jerusalem. Verses 7-8 form the
introduction and first strophe, and contain the familiar words,
"How beautiful upon the mountains are the feet of him who
brings good tidings, who publishes peace . . . who says to Zion,
'Your God reigns.'" The Exile is over, and in the people's
pilgrimage to Zion the Lord will go before them and will also
be their rear guard as he was in the wandering through the
wilderness in the days of Moses. The return to Zion is described
in terms of a great pilgrimage to the Holy City and also as a
great victory of God over all those who have opposed him.
These same themes were central in certain Temple services of
worship in pre-exilic Jerusalem.

The mood of the prophet in this hymn is triumphant and
excited, and here he brings to a climax his proclamations of the
coming of the Lord and of the release of the exiles and the
rebuilding of the Holy City, Zion.

The Lord's Suffering Servant (52:13—53:12)

This is the most familiar passage in Second Isaiah. The subject is the atoning or reconciling work of the Servant in the world. The redemption of Israel is represented as having been completed. The Servant has been commissioned (49:5-6) and has acknowledged the work of the Lord and accepted the Lord's guidance (50:4-9). The Servant's suffering and affliction in the world continue, but as this prophetic poem eloquently explains, they are for the sake of others. The Servant voluntarily will take upon himself the punishment merited by others. The picture is startling, dramatic, and very personal. Its features have caused much debate over the centuries concerning its meaning and the designation of the Servant. Jewish scholarship has generally interpreted the passage as referring to the sufferings of Israel in the world. Christian scholarship has interpreted the passage as referring to Christ. Indeed, in the New Testament a very original modification of the Jewish expectation of the Messiah was made in terms of this passage. As is clear from 9:2-7 and 11:1-9, the promise of God to David had become for Israel the hope that God would provide a new David on the throne in Jerusalem who would serve as God's ruler over the whole world in the time of the Kingdom of God. The Early Church, however, saw Jesus in his life and death as fulfilling this prophecy of the Suffering Servant, and as fulfilling in his exaltation after death the prophecies about the new Davidic ruler. Thus the kingship of the Messiah is exercised from the heavenly throne, it is a spiritual lordship over the world (Acts 8:31-35; Rom. 15:21; I Peter 2:21-25).

Modern biblical scholarship has in general followed Jewish interpretation, at least in seeing the Servant here and in the earlier passages in Second Isaiah as a collective concept and referring to the redeemed Israel. Yet this prophecy has never played a central role in Jewish theology or expectation in the same sense that it has for Christianity. In recent times there have been attempts to see in the Suffering Servant an idealized Messianic figure, or else to see in the poem a portion of a liturgy which depicted the humiliation of the current reigning king before his exaltation. For the reasons specified in the study of the earlier chapters, and in particular of the Servant references, the collective interpretation of the original poem seems preferable. Israel as God's servant is vicariously bearing the sins of the world. This vicarious atonement is the means whereby the nations are led to the Lord. Christian faith, however, sees this vocation of Israel dramatically fulfilled in Christ.

The poem falls into three main parts. In the first (52:13-15), God announces the exaltation and success of the Servant's mission. In the second and major part (53:1-9), the kings of the nations confess their understanding of the Servant's sufferings. Finally, in the third section (53:10-12), the prophet announces that the sufferings are by the will of the Lord and that their purpose will be fulfilled. In verse 12 the prophet quotes God directly as speaking again of the Servant's future exaltation.

God's Introduction and Exaltation of the Servant (52:13-15)

The first strophe begins in verse 13 with a summary statement in which God is represented as speaking in the first person. It announces that the Servant is to have great success in his mission and that as a result there will be a radical change from his present low estate to a very high one. Indeed, it is going to come about that, just as many people were surprised to see how his body was marked with wounds and stripes beyond those of normal men, in the future kings will be put to silence by their understanding of the magnitude and remarkable nature of the work and life which the Servant has carried on. Things that kings had never been told and had never heard, they will now see and understand (vss. 14-15). In the first line of verse 15, the meaning of the Hebrew word translated "startle" is not clear. What the prophet means, however, is to be understood from its parallelism with the first line of verse 14 and its context in verse 15. As people were surprised to see such a marred and ugly figure, so they are going to be surprised when they understand the meaning of his person. Thus the phrase "kings shall shut their mouths" must include something of the thought that is involved in the unknown Hebrew word. Some new information about the Servant is going to come to the nations of the world, information which hitherto they have not possessed.

The Confession of the Kings of the Nations (53:1-9)

This descriptive and confessional section is introduced ab-

ruptly and speaks of the Servant of the Lord in the third person.
It is composed of three strophes, verses 1-3, 4-6, and 7-9. It
begins with the question, "Who has believed what we have
heard? And to whom has the arm of the LORD been revealed?"
To interpret the passage we need to know the identity of the
speaker and of the message that has been heard. This is an
age-old problem, as we see in the questions asked the evangelist
Philip by the Ethiopian eunuch (Acts 8:34). A common assumption has been that it is indeed the prophet who is speaking,
as the Ethiopian eunuch suggested. Another comparatively recent
suggestion sees the servant poems as taken from an Israelite
version of a Babylonian New Year's liturgy concerned with the
humiliation and the exaltation of the reigning king. As a quotation from royal liturgy, the poem then in a derived sense
could be spoken of as Messianic. The simplest and most direct
explanation, however, and the one given by what is probably a
majority of interpreters today, is that 53:1-3 is very closely
related to the preceding strophe (52:13-15) and that the
speakers are the kings of the nations mentioned in verse 15.
The information which they had not known or heard they now
see and understand. It is the revelation from God himself about
the meaning of what has been going on. The answer to the
question in 53:1 is that no one could have believed what we
have heard, and to no one hitherto had its meaning been revealed. Verse 2 is closely paralleled by 52:14. The outward appearance of the Servant is so unattractive as to make him repulsive; he is one at whom nobody desires to look. Those who
find a clear Messianic allusion in the first part of verse 2 think
the phrases "a young plant" and "a root out of dry ground"
refer to the "shoot from the stump" of the household of David's
father, Jesse (11:1). That this is meant, however, seems rather
problematical. Verse 3 specifies in more detail the situation of
the Servant of the Lord. He was an outcast from society, despised, and without friends. He was a man of "sorrows" and
"grief" (literally, "pains" and "sickness"). The Servant was
such an unattractive and diseased creature that men could not
bear to look at him: "we esteemed him not." There comes to
mind at this point an eloquent passage in Job 12:5, "In the
thought of one who is at ease there is contempt for misfortune."
Those who are well and healthy find it easy to look down on
and to despise those who are unhealthy, ugly, diseased. While

we may fight the tendency to do this, it seems to be an attitude against which indeed we must struggle. The Servant is pictured as ugly, diseased, lonely, and unwanted.

In the second strophe the kings of the world now confess the understanding that has been revealed to them about the real meaning of the sufferings of the Servant. While they thought him to be simply stricken and afflicted and for some reason "smitten by God," they confess that of a truth he is indeed bearing "our griefs" and "our sorrows." Verse 5 now changes the metaphor. "He was wounded for our transgressions" means that it was "because of" or "on account of" the evil of the world that he was wounded. It would be a common and widespread notion in ancient Israel, as in the ancient world generally, that such a one as the Servant who is here depicted was indeed a man afflicted because of sin. Yet it is not his sin which is in question, but the sins of the peoples of the world. His body bears the marks of that sin, yet at the same time his bearing of these wounds was for purposes of atonement, that is, for reconciliation with God: "with his stripes we are healed." The Servant is bearing the evil of the world vicariously. It should not be forgotten that every human being bears his share of the world's evil. A very special and unusual weight of it was heaped upon this Servant; but he accepted the burden and bore it as his mission in the world. It is for this reason that Christians have always associated Christ with this passage; the New Testament interpretation of his crucifixion, in fact, is made in similar terms. His was not a martyrdom but a vicarious suffering for the healing of the nations.

In verse 6 the world rulers continue their confession: every one of us has strayed like lost sheep, and the Lord has laid on him the burden of our alienation. Note the emphasis on "All we" at the beginning of verse 6, and also on "the LORD," who has laid on the Servant this burden of the world's evil (see vs. 10).

The third strophe of the confession of the kings interprets the life of the Servant (vss. 7-9). As in 42:2-3 he is quietly and without complaint obedient; like a lamb or a sheep led to its slaughter or its shearers, the Servant does not make a sound. In verses 8-9 the picture is of a death and a burial along with the evil people of the world, although the Servant has done nothing whatsoever to deserve the death. The picture can be looked at in a double way. On the one hand, it may be seen as a mirror of the destruction of the Israelite nation in the Promised Land. On the other, it may be looked at as the fate of God's Servant in the world, who vicariously bears in his body the world's evil. Here again it is easy to see how and why Christians have found in these words an understanding of the sufferings of Christ.

God's Description of the Servant's Atoning Work (53:10-12)

In verses 10-11 the prophet in his own words explains the life of the Servant in terms of the purposive action of God, a purpose which the Servant has of his own will carried out. It was according to God's active will that he was wounded and made sick. Yet in the future he will see a family, a prolongation of days, and a prospering that were denied him in the past. The meaning of verse 11 has been somewhat debated because of the ambiguity of the Hebrew. Yet the general intention of the words is clear. By the work of the Servant many shall "be accounted righteous" (a technical phrase for an acquittal in a lawsuit). Finally we are told that because the Servant "poured out his soul to death" (vs. 12) and was willing to be numbered with sinners, while bearing their sins and making intercession for them, therefore God, now speaking in the first person, will divide for him a portion with the greatest ones of the earth. The figure in the first part of the verse is that of the general of a great army after a victory, parceling out the booty to the strongest and best of the warriors. The despised and lonely Servant will obtain a portion reserved for the greatest and strongest of all warriors.

In this picture of the Suffering Servant we find a portrayal of Israel's meaning and destiny in the world that rises far above its own horizon and points to a larger reference in later times and situations. Thus it was with Israel in the original picture; thus it was also with Christians who saw Christ exactly prefigured in this figure of the Servant; and thus it has been with the New Israel in Christ and with its mission in the world in all times and places.

"Your Maker Is Your Husband" (54:1-17)

Chapter 54 represents an abrupt change of theme, and it

contains no hint of the great climax that has been reached in the preceding chapter. Whether this effect was designed purposely by Second Isaiah himself, or whether it is the work of the prophet's disciples who transmitted his prophecies, we do not know. On the whole one must say that there is an inner logic in the arrangement of the materials in Second Isaiah which we have examined so far. This is very unusual in prophecy, and leads to the supposition that the original prophet may well have had a hand in the arrangement of his poems. But of this we simply cannot be sure.

Chapter 54 can perhaps be considered as another recapitulation. A climax has been reached, and now the prophet looks back and in a fresh way repeats a number of old themes which he has treated before. It will thus be an interlude before the next climax is reached in chapter 55.

The theme of chapter 54 is the encouragement of Israel, with the repeated exhortation not to fear. Note the emphasis in verse 7: "For a brief moment I forsook you, but with great compassion I will gather you." The metaphorical language which the prophet uses, however, reaches back to the prophecy of Hosea, where the Covenant between God and Israel is compared to a marriage covenant; Israel is the wife who has been faithless (Hosea 1-2). Here, however, the metaphor is used in an entirely fresh way. In the first strophe (vss. 1-3), Israel is a wife who has not been producing children. That kind of barrenness is now over. Many children are to be born, and the family tents will have to be enlarged.

In verses 4-10 the nation is addressed. The "shame" of her youth and the "reproach" of her widowhood are now over. God has espoused her to himself. "Your Maker is your husband . . . and the Holy One of Israel is your Redeemer," declares the prophet (vs. 5). Verse 6 continues the metaphor: here the reference is to the sad thing that evidently happened not infrequently in polygamous societies and still happens in modern Arab countries. "A wife of youth"—that is, one's first wife—becomes old and ceases to bear children. The husband then takes himself a younger wife, leaving the older one forsaken. In the case of Israel, God has now called to her as to a wife who had once been forsaken. Verse 9 makes reference to the covenant with Noah (Gen. 9:8-17). That covenant contained the promise that never again would there be a threat of flood waters covering the whole earth. God's "covenant of peace" with Israel is to be just as firm a commitment and as everlasting as was that with Noah (vs. 10). The final portion of the chapter (vss. 11-17) continues this assurance but uses a new metaphor, that of the building of a city. The city will be one made of "precious stones" (vs. 12). The children will all be taught by the Lord, and no one will need to have fear, for the Lord will be their protector.

Invitation to the Banquet of the Lord (55:1-13)

This chapter contains the final poem and the climax of the prophecies of Second Isaiah which were composed about 540 B.C., shortly before the Persian conquest of the Babylonian empire in 539 B.C. (see Introduction to Isaiah 40-66). In its theme and its triumphant, elevated style the poem gives every evidence of having been intended as the conclusion and climax of this series of prophecies. In the first three strophes (vss. 1-2, 3-5, 6-9) note the prominence of imperatives: "Come," "hearken," "incline your ear," "seek." Each of the last two strophes (vss. 10-11, 12-13) begins with the word "for." The Hebrew in this case does not have the meaning of "because" but is rather a strong asseveration: "surely," or "of a truth." Thus the imperatives are followed by an expression of certainties.

Verses 1-5 issue an eloquent invitation to the Messianic banquet for all peoples, the banquet of the Kingdom of God (see also 25:6-7). The thought is that in the days to come, when the alienation of mankind and of God's own people will have been healed, then there will be a great banquet or Covenant meal, with all mankind present and God's Messiah presiding at the head of the table. This expectation became very prominent in Intertestament Judaism among the Essenes of the Dead Sea community and in the New Testament Church. The Lord's Supper in the latter and the daily meals at Qumran thus became communion banquets looking forward to the great banquet of the Kingdom when the Messiah would be present (see Mark 14:25; Luke 22:14-20; I Cor. 11:26).

The invitation in verse 1 is addressed to everyone who is thirsty and hungry. It is a free meal. Then comes the challenging question in verse 2 as to why people spend so much money for food that is not satisfying. Come instead to the banquet of the Lord and enjoy the finest of good things!

In verses 3-5 there is a reference to God's everlasting Covenant with David; that is, to the Messianic thought of Israel. The promises contained in that Covenant will be completely fulfilled in the age about to dawn. For references to this Covenant see II Samuel 7:8-16; 23:5; Psalm 89:3-4, 9-37, 49. The words "my steadfast, sure love for David" refer to God's Covenant promises to David which are to be realized and fulfilled in the new era. In verses 4-5 the new David, God's Messiah, is to be the leader of mankind, a "witness" to all people, so that as a result the nations of the world will flock to Israel because of the Lord their God. That is, as in the New Testament the salvation of all mankind is to come through God's act in Jesus Christ, so here the salvation of mankind comes through the revelation of God in Israel, the Messianic king being his agent. The use of the term "witness" for the Messiah is unusual. The prophet's reference to Cyrus as God's "messiah" ("anointed") in 45:1, and his emphasis on the saving role of Israel as God's servant, means that he has not emphasized the role of God's king from the line of David in the new day, as did First Isaiah in 9:1-6; 11:1-9. Warlike metaphors are used only in connection with God's punishing work through Cyrus; Second Isaiah does not use them in relation to Israel as God's servant nor in this single reference to the Davidic Messiah.

The invitation to the Covenant banquet is accompanied by the great invitation to come to the Lord in repentance, for the Lord is ready to have mercy (vss. 6-9). His thoughts and ways are far greater in understanding than ours. Let all men, therefore, forsake their ways and turn unto the Lord to receive his mercy and forgiveness.

The fourth strophe (vss. 10-11) uses the metaphor of the seasons as a way of expressing the certainty and stability of the word of the Lord. God's word is his purpose, and it will accomplish the thing for which God sends it into the world. The final strophe (vss. 12-13) returns to the scene of the new Exodus and to the joy of the whole creation in this great event. Nature will be transformed, and that transformation will be a memorial to the great work of the Lord, "an everlasting sign which shall not be cut off."

The beauty and the richness of the words in this chapter

have sung themselves into human hearts through the ages; they are among the most familiar in the whole Bible. They perfectly express our hope in the Lord, which is our hope for the future.

PROPHECIES FROM THE REBUILT JERUSALEM
Isaiah 56:1—66:24

This final section of the Isaiah literature comes mostly from a time when the city of Jerusalem has been rebuilt, as has also the Temple (see Introduction to Isaiah 40-66). The author or authors of these chapters are in Jerusalem, and allusion is made to life in the revived city. The spirit of Second Isaiah so infuses the chapters that it seems impossible to attribute them to a "Third Isaiah" as has frequently been done in the past. It is more appropriate to see this material as deriving from the school of Second Isaiah, most of it indeed from the inspiration of the prophet himself, although perhaps his disciples in this case have played an important role in the actual composition as well as in the transmission of the prophecy. The chapters seem to divide themselves into two main groups, 56-59 and 60-66, the second group having to do almost solely with the coming age of complete restoration for Israel and the conversion of the world in the new age which, according to the prophet's perspective, was about to dawn. That is, the restoration of Jerusalem, its Temple, and a small province of Judah in the years between 539 and 515 B.C. have not brought the complete fulfillment predicted in chapters 40-55. The hope for the future, however, still burns brightly as a vital part of faith in the Lord.

Divine Exhortation (56:1—59:21)

God's Promise to Society's Outcasts (56:1-8)

We now come to material that is very different in mood and in type from that encountered in chapters 40-55. The form is not that of prophecy but of exhortation concerned with worship in the rebuilt Temple (vs. 7). This is one of the reasons why many interpreters have assumed that this section must have been written by an author other than Second Isaiah himself. Another reason for the assumption of a different authorship is the reference to Sabbath-keeping in verse 2. Second Isaiah in chapters 40-55 says nothing about such details of the religious life. The real question to be asked, however, is whether the changed situation cannot account for the change in mood. Since the Temple has been rebuilt and worship is going on within it, the time of composition must be after 515 B.C., when the Temple was completed, and therefore at least a quarter of a century later than the composition of chapters 40-55. Certainly the great-mindedness, the compassion, and the interest in all mankind shown in verses 3-8 is directly within the spirit of the earlier prophecy.

The exhortation begins with the command to keep justice and to do righteousness, for the salvation of God is soon to come. That is, in the interim of waiting, high standards of ethical community life must be maintained. Verse 2 is in the form of a saying popular among the wise men of Israel, and not common in prophecy. The Hebrew word at the beginning of the verse is mistakenly translated "blessed." The Hebrew word refers rather to the fortunate or happy state of the person who has received blessing, not to the act of blessing itself. Hence the meaning here is "fortunate is the man who does this"; that is, who acts with justice and righteousness in his dealings with others. The phrase "son of man" simply means "human being" and is used by the Hebrew poet who does not wish to repeat the word "man" in a poetic line with synonymous parallelism between the two parts of it. Responsible, ethical life includes the keeping of the Sabbath as a holy day, it being an institution set within the divinely created order (Gen. 2:1-3) and an integral part of the Mosaic Covenant as indicated by the Decalogue (Exod. 20:8-11). Since it is the only institution specifically mentioned in the Decalogue, it is impossible to assume that it was not a matter of great importance to the Israelite religious leader, whether prophet, priest, or Levitical teacher. Israel was the first people of the world to see the seven-day week as a part of God's creative order, with one of those days separated as a day of rest and worship. The institution was to be widely adopted in the Roman empire, even among those who cared nothing for the Jewish or Christian religions.

In verses 3-8 we have one of the finest and most compassionate statements in the whole of Scripture. When foreigners are converted and join in the common worship of God in the Temple, there is to be absolutely no segregation whatsoever. All are to join joyfully in the services, for the Temple "shall be called a house of prayer for all peoples" (vs. 7). In verse 8 the Lord is quoted as declaring that he is going to gather to himself people other than those of Israel. The Bible has often been used wrongly by proponents of racial segregation in modern times, but this passage in the spirit and from the school of Israel's greatest prophet is the most forthright statement possible against any artificial divisions among those whom God chooses to make his own people. The relation of Gentiles to Jews was a continuing problem in Judaism and was the first major controversy within the early Christian community, one that was settled as the school of Second Isaiah would have had it settled (see Acts 15). When Jesus cleansed the Temple he coupled the passage about God's house as a house of prayer with the reference to a cave of robbers in Jeremiah 7:11, as a statement of what the Temple really was supposed to be in contrast to what it had become (Mark 11:17).

The parallel message to the eunuchs (vss. 3-5) is remarkable. Israelites had a great respect for the body as a creation of God and therefore had a horror of bodily mutilation. According to old Hebrew law, a eunuch could not be a full member of the community of Israel or of the community of worship (Deut. 23:1). Yet in the course of the centuries, and especially in the Persian government, many who took offices in the royal palace were forced to become eunuchs in order to maintain their positions. Here the eunuch is specifically addressed by God and told that special provision will be made for him within the Temple and that he will be given a monument better than the family which he cannot have. This indeed is a marvelous and comforting saying to people caught within the ways of the world, and who otherwise might suffer a kind of separation and excommunication from their communities.

Condemnation of Corrupt Leaders (56:9—57:13)

This section suddenly introduces a type of condemnation like that found in First Isaiah and other pre-exilic prophets. It is clear that the suffering and exile of Israel have taught some of the people nothing whatever. Consequently among the new community are "watchmen" (prophets and religious leaders) and "shepherds" (community leaders, government officials) who are called greedy "dogs" (vs. 11). The irresponsible use of strong drink (vs. 12) reminds one of similar words in 5:11, 22.

In 57:1-10 a group of the community are condemned in the strongest possible terms. They are idolators and are also unjust in their relations to their fellows, so that the righteous and the devout are not safe from their actions. The identity of this group is unknown, but it is the first time in the literature of Second Isaiah that such a forthright condemnation in the name of God is addressed to a specific group of people, other than the taunt song against Babylon in chapter 47. This section, then, is the clearest possible indication of the changed situation behind the prophecy. A new community in Palestine has been formed, and there are those within it who have learned nothing from their past.

In verses 11-13 the judgment upon these people is pronounced. When it comes, their collection of idols will not be able to deliver them, for the idols are so light and insignificant that a wind will carry them away. The ones who are to possess this land, meaning the Promised Land of Palestine, are those— and only those—who take refuge in the Lord.

God's Promise to the Humble and Contrite (57:14-21)

It is not improbable that verses 14-21 are simply a continuation of the preceding poem. The promise of restoration, guidance, and peace to those who take refuge in the Lord (see end of vs. 13) is now elaborated. God is high and lofty; he has eternity as his place of abode, and Holy is his name. Nevertheless, he is a God who is with the humble and the contrite in spirit (vs. 15). Indeed, the spirit which gives life comes solely from him (vs. 16).

The theme in verses 16-19, that God punished his people in the past because of their backsliding but that now he proposes to heal them and bring peace to those far and near, has been developed in the earlier chapters (see, for example, 42:18— 43:7; 48:8-11; 51:17-23; 54:7-10). For this healing, which would remove the infection that had led them to rebel against their Lord, Israel hoped devoutly. It was an integral part of her hope for the great age to come that God would remove this disease, the root evil so frequently described in the pages of the Bible, as for example in the story of the first man and woman (Gen. 3; see also Jer. 31:31-34; Ezek. 36:22-32). The urgency of this desire for cleansing appears also as an important part of the great psalm of confession (Ps. 51:6-12). The center of the New Testament is directed squarely at this basic problem. The meaning of God's act in Jesus Christ is understood as the deliverance of man from the burden of his sin and the provision of the possibility of a new life apart from that slavery.

The final verses (20-21) deal with the wicked who have been described in the preceding section. In God's plan there is no future for such people. They are like the tossing sea which is continually stirring up "mire and dirt," but "there is no peace . . . for the wicked." Verse 21 seems to be in its proper context here (see comment on 48:22).

The Meaning of True Fasting (58:1-14)

The exhortation in this chapter is comparable in intensity and condemnation to the earlier prophecy delivered before the fall of Jerusalem. It deals with the question of what true worship involves and repudiates the shallowness of a religious observance which is regarded as fulfilling the desire of the Deity while leaving the daily life of the community completely unaffected (compare 1:10-20; Amos 5:21-24; Micah 6:1-8). Yet the wording here is fresh, penetrating, and original. It is also to be noted that in form this poem is largely exhortation and explanation, while the form of earlier prophecy dealing with the sin of Israel is that of a messenger's report on the decree of the heavenly Judge concerning the trial and sentencing of Israel as God's vassal people (see Introduction to Isaiah 1-39).

The poem begins with God's summoning the prophet to make a proclamation to the house of Jacob concerning their sins (vs. 1). Of course, the people are going to be hard to convince of this fact (vs. 2). As a nation they are very faithful in the worship of God, who declares, "They seek me daily, and delight to know my ways . . . they delight to draw near to God." When they are told that they are sinners, they are going to reply in effect: "Have you not seen how we have fasted and humbled ourselves?" That is, "Have you not noticed what excellent worshipers we are?" In times of national peril or trouble, ritual fasting had always been the accustomed thing in

Israel. We know that after the fall of Jerusalem and the destruction of the Temple by the Babylonians in 587 (or 586) B.C.,
regular services of fasting and mourning were carried on at
the site of the former Temple. Jeremiah 41:4-5 refers to people
from Shechem, Shiloh, and Samaria going on a pilgrimage to
Jerusalem in deep mourning. This mourning and fasting for the
Temple is also referred to in Zechariah 7:2-7 and 8:19. Mourning for the fall of Jerusalem and its Temple was evidently one
dominant theme of the worship in the exilic and postexilic
periods. In Isaiah 58, however, it is probable that the term
"fast" is simply a short way of speaking about the external forms
of religious worship in the revived community of the early
postexilic period.

Beginning with the word "Behold" in the second half of
verse 3 and continuing through verse 5, the prophet, or God
through the prophet, exposes the shallowness of this worship
which the people take to be sufficient. In their fasting the people
have no interest in what God really wants of them, nor have
they any interest in the needs of their fellow men. Are their fast
days going to be acceptable to the Lord, and will the Lord listen
to their prayers, if all they have done is put on the formal
trappings of humility while they continue to quarrel and fight
among themselves and to oppress the people who work for
them?

In verses 6-7 God's true fast is explained in terms of the
classic Hebrew doctrine of righteousness. That is, as God used
his great power to save Israel from slavery in Egypt, so the
strong and responsible citizens among God's people should use
their power "to let the oppressed go free" and "to share . . .
bread with the hungry." True fasting is to "loose the bonds of
wickedness" which harm and enslave others. The formal rites
of fasting mean nothing if the common life of those who fast
does not reflect the righteousness of God. Like First Isaiah, the
prophet regards a worship that is separated from righteousness
in the common life as a worship which God hates (see 1:14).
Prayers offered by people who keep the spheres of religion
and common life separate will not be heard by the Lord.

Beginning in verse 8, the consequences of a sincere fast that
has radical consequences in the common life are developed.
In the second half of the verse, the figure of the glory of God

leading the people through the wilderness is used. The phrase "your righteousness" is in synonymous parallelism with "the glory of the LORD" and is a divine title (for the figure see Num. 10:34; compare Exod. 16:7, 10). In its literal sense "the glory of the LORD" meant a cloud or a brilliant light which surrounded God so that he could not be seen by the human eye. Yet the presence of God is certain whenever his glory is seen. The striking figure enabled the Israelite to express the certainty of God's presence, while at the same time preserving the sense of the mystery of his holiness into which man cannot penetrate.

In the concluding verses of chapter 58, God's promise of his protecting presence and guidance and of the rebuilding of the "ancient ruins" is made conditional upon righteousness in personal and corporate life. In verses 13-14 the prophet turns again to the Sabbath, as in 56:2. Some commentators in the past have felt this to be too prosaic and mundane a matter for so great a spirit as Second Isaiah and that this concern with the Sabbath indicates a smallness of heart on the part of another author or authors of these chapters. This is a mistake in judgment (see also the comment on 56:1-8). Taking seriously the Sabbath as "the holy day of the LORD" is not meant by the prophet as a mere legalistic observance. Instead he is talking about a religious observance which gives expression to the people's loyalty and delight in the Lord. The phrase in verse 14, "I will make you ride upon the heights of the earth," is a metaphor reminiscent of Canaanite mythology. The figure is that of a dragon in charge of the underworld, and to "ride upon" his back was a way of speaking about taming or conquering him (see also Deut. 32:13; 33:29; II Sam. 22:34; Ps. 18:33). Thus "heights" probably originally meant "back," though it is not improbable that the original signification of the allusion may have been forgotten in Israel by the time of Second Isaiah. In any event, it is an old metaphorical expression for exaltation and security.

"The Lord's Hand Is Not Shortened" (59:1-21)

Chapter 59 is a new exposition and exhortation dealing with the unredeemed life of the new community in Jerusalem. The great age of God has not come, even though a community of exiles has returned and has been rebuilding the ruins. Why has God not come? In the first section of this exposition (vss. 1-8) the prophet explains the reason. It is not that the Lord's hand does not have enough power to save nor that his ear is too dull to hear the prayers of the people. It is that their evil has created a gulf between himself and them. In verses 3-8 the deeds of the community which are violations of the will of God are specified in some detail. The final verses of the section eloquently summarize: "Their feet run to evil . . . The way of peace they know not, and there is no justice in their paths; they have made their roads crooked, no one who goes in them knows peace." Here we have the same explanation of trouble in the body politic that was given by the pre-exilic prophets. There can be no peace and salvation so long as there is personal and community evil. It is characteristic of human beings to desire peace apart from judgment, apart from their accountability for the society they have produced and for the actions of that society. But, "There is no peace . . . for the wicked" (57:21).

The second section of the poem (vss. 9-15) is as eloquent as the preceding. Indeed, if this passage is not by Second Isaiah himself, we would have to presume that it is by a disciple who shared his great gifts, both of theological insight and of skill in the use of words.

It is because of the separation between God and people brought about by the people's sinful acts that the community of Jerusalem "look for light, and behold, darkness, and for brightness, but . . . walk in gloom" (vs. 9). The word for "look" can also be translated "wait," and the word for "gloom" means "blackness." The structure reminds us strongly of one of Jeremiah's expressions: "We looked for peace, but no good came, for a time of healing, but behold, terror" (Jer. 8:15). Another use of light as a term for salvation, and of darkness for its opposite, appears in 60:1-3.

Whereas the first section is in the form of an explanatory declaration to Israel about her sin, the second section is in the form of a confession. The prophet on behalf of the people confesses: ". . . our transgressions are multiplied before thee, and our sins testify against us" (vs. 12). This is the reason "Justice is turned back . . . for truth has fallen in the public squares . . . Truth is lacking, and he who departs from evil makes himself a prey" (vss. 14-15). The word "truth" is used here in a typically Hebraic manner. It derives from the same verbal root as do words for reliability, faith, and faithfulness. It refers to fidelity to God's will and is used in verse 14 in synonymous parallelism with justice, righteousness, and uprightness. The picture of the prophet as intercessor for his people is most clearly illustrated in Jeremiah. (See his prayer of confession in Jeremiah 14:7-9, and note also 14:10—15:1 for a colloquy between Jeremiah and the Lord concerning the prophet's intercession in behalf of his people.) Intercession was not a priestly function in Israel; it was part of the work of the prophet. As God's appointed representative on earth, he was in a special position to represent the people before God. Israel in looking back upon the figure of Moses saw him as a prophet who interceded on the people's behalf repeatedly (for example, Num. 11-12 and 14).

The final section of the poem begins in the second half of verse 15 and continues through verse 21. Here God is pictured as the warrior who himself actively takes up the war against sin and evil in the world. Because of this, man can have hope. What man cannot do in reforming his life, God will accomplish. The picture of God as warrior is a very common one in the Old Testament. As the sovereign Ruler of the world, his activity in behalf of his own causes and against those who would thwart his purpose is spoken of in political terms as a warfare, and he is described as leading his forces in battle. This metaphor is by no means in opposition to the other pictures of God as the active Judge of the world and as the Father and the Shepherd of his people. All were functions of kingship. The picture of God as warrior is a particularly dynamic one because it shows him in intensely active combat against the sin and evil of the world. This, then, is the real ground of man's faith, trust, and hope. The picture continues in the New Testament, where in the background of history God and his heavenly hosts are represented as in conflict with Satan and the powers of darkness, a conflict that will be resolved with Satan's defeat and the triumph of the rule of God.

In verses 16-17 God is represented as putting on the armor of the warrior after seeing that there was no one on earth who would take up arms against human evil. This figure of the armor of God is elaborated in the familiar passage in Ephesians 6:13-17. The passage in Ephesians adds to the "breastplate of righteousness" and the "helmet of salvation" the "shield of faith" and the "sword of the Spirit." The "garments of vengeance

for clothing" in Isaiah refer not to an unworthy attribute of
God, but to God as the one who is responsible for the adminis-
tration of justice in the world. As has been noted, the English
word "vengeance," with its solely negative connotation in our
time, is simply an improper rendering of the Hebrew. The
Hebrew term refers to God's vindication of his cause, whether
it is judgment upon his enemies or salvation for those who
love him.

The final verse of the poem pictures the return of the Lord
to Zion in triumph as Redeemer (vs. 20). It is possible that
verse 21 was added by a compiler; nevertheless, it is profound in
its thought. God's Covenant with his people—that is, his way
of relating himself to them—is here described. The Spirit of the
Lord, that empowering by God within the mind and soul of
man, is upon his people and he has put his words in their
mouths, and they shall not depart from the people or from their
children forever. The possession of the Spirit and the word in
man's innermost being is God's eternal Covenant. The thought
is comparable to Jeremiah's "new covenant" which envisages
God's law written upon the hearts of his people so that they
will no longer need to teach one another about the Lord, for
all shall know him, from the youngest to the eldest (Jer. 31:31-
34).

"Arise, Shine; for Your Light Has Come" (60:1—66:24)

The Lord, Your Everlasting Light (60:1-22)

The school of Second Isaiah has collected in the last seven
chapters of the book a group of marvelous eschatological poems,
of which chapter 60 is one of the most beautiful. The dominant
theme in chapters 56-59 was judgment, for the life in the new
community had not given evidence of the new age of glory.
Consequently, only one part of the eschatological program en-
visioned by Second Isaiah (chs. 40-55) had been fulfilled—the
release by Cyrus of all exiles who wished to return to their
homeland. The exhortations in chapters 56-59, therefore, are
more in the nature of admonitions, exhortations, and interpre-
tations of both current life and the will of the Lord. Beginning
with chapter 60 the vigor and exaltation characteristic of chap-

ters 40-55 are again present, as the prophet presents the picture of the coming glory of God.

The poem begins with a marvelous use of the figure of light and darkness (vss. 1-3). Although darkness covers the earth, the glory of the Lord as a brilliant light will arise on Israel, and nations shall stream out of the darkness into the light which shines so brightly in Jerusalem. The prophet then asks the people in their imagination to lift their eyes round about to observe their own sons and daughters coming from afar, being gathered together again in the Promised Land. Then the wealth of the nations shall stream to Jerusalem as mankind arrives to "proclaim the praise of the LORD," with the result that the Temple will become a glorious building (vss. 4-7). The prophet Haggai, during the time when the Temple was being built, had expressed a similar thought. To those who felt disappointed by the poverty of the new buildings erected between 520 and 515 B.C. he said that in due course all nations would contribute their wealth to the building, so that it would be filled with splendor (Haggai 2:1-9).

Among the peoples who are mentioned as making the pilgrimage to Jerusalem are those of Arabia (vss. 6-7). The Phoenician ships which ply the Mediterranean, in particular the "Tarshish" or refinery ships, will bring not only Israel's sons but also silver and gold for the honor of the name of the Holy One of Israel (vss. 8-9).

Verses 10-14 are concerned with the building up of the fortifications of the ancient city. The task will be performed by foreigners. The wood of the Lebanon Mountains, so much desired by the kings of the whole Near East for temple buildings, will be used to beautify the Temple in Jerusalem. People who had formerly despised Israel will now come and bow before the city and name it "the City of the LORD, the Zion of the Holy One of Israel" (vs. 14). The problem of stating properly this glorification of Israel and Jerusalem by the nations of the world is a very difficult one. The glorification of God because of his saving work and his use of his servant as his witness before mankind in the world is a prominent theme throughout the literature of Second Isaiah. In verses 12 and 15-16, however, the expressions verge on the nationalistic and seem to be some distance removed from the conception of the Suffering Servant in chapter 53. The destruction of the nations that will

not serve Israel (vs. 12) may indeed be according to the plan
of God, but not so much because they will not serve Israel as
because they will not serve God himself.

The final verses of the chapter begin with a beautiful picture
of a land at peace: "I will make your overseers peace and your
taskmasters righteousness. Violence shall no more be heard in
your land . . . you shall call your walls Salvation, and your
gates Praise" (vss. 17-18). The author then turns again to the
figure of light with which the chapter began. There will be no
further need for the sun and the moon to give light by day and
by night because the Lord will be for the people an everlasting
light (vss. 19-20). Revelation 21:22-26 repeats this scene and
others in this chapter, including the conception of a light so
brilliant that it will draw all nations to the New Jerusalem, where
the gates of the city will never be shut, either by day or by
night (see Isa. 60:11). Living in the light of the Lord, the
people of Israel "shall all be righteous; they shall possess the
land for ever," and even the smallest one will be important in
God's scheme of things.

"You Shall Be . . . Ministers of Our God" (61:1-11)

The poem in this chapter is best known for the first three
verses, part of which Jesus read in the synagogue in Nazareth
and then applied to himself (Luke 4:16-19). How the prophet
meant them to be understood is not entirely clear in the present
context. Does the first verse, "The Spirit of the Lord GOD is upon
me, because the LORD has anointed me to bring good tidings to
the afflicted . . ." refer to the prophet himself or is this another
servant poem comparable to those in chapters 42, 49, 50, and
53? The concept of the Spirit of the Lord coming upon a prophet
in order to inspire him and make him capable of performing his
mission is a common feature of the prophetic self-consciousness.
During the monarchy the office of the prophet was successor
to the leadership designated by the gift of the Spirit in the days
of the tribal league. By his Spirit God raised up the prophets to
see to it that his word was heard by both king and people. It
was when the Spirit of the Lord came upon a prophet that he
prophesied (Num. 11:26-29; 24:2-3; I Sam. 10:6, 10). It is
commonly thought that the pre-exilic prophets whose works
are preserved in the Scripture generally avoided the use of the
term "spirit" in connection with their own missions, because of

its close association in the popular mind with the false prophets and ecstatic activity. Nevertheless, it is certain that the prophets were conceived as men empowered by the Spirit of God (see also Micah 3:8). Furthermore, while the word "anoint" is not generally associated with the office of prophecy, Psalm 105:15 could be interpreted as applying the term to the prophets, though it is more probable that even there it may refer to the anointed leaders of the nation, either the kings alone or the kings and the priests.

It appears that a stronger case can be made for the supposition that the passage is referring to Israel as God's Servant. Note that verse 10 within the same poem may also refer to the Servant who has been clothed "with the garments of salvation." That the Servant is empowered by God's Spirit has already been affirmed in 42:1. The association of the act of anointing with the coming of the Spirit is to be noticed not only in the anointing of Saul (I Sam. 10:1-12) but also in the anointing of David as king (I Sam. 16:13; II Sam. 23:1-2). Whether the word "anointed" is applied to the prophet or to Israel as the Servant of the Lord, this is in either case an extended use of it, as is also true of its use in 45:1 (see comment). That the Servant People have a prophetic role to play in the world as God's messengers and spokesmen has already been made clear in the preceding servant poems in chapters 40-55. Most convincing, however, is the fact that the task of the Servant in the preceding poems is precisely what it is specified to be in these verses: to bring the gospel of God's salvation to the afflicted, to set captives at liberty, and to bring comfort and joy to all who are in trouble, to the end that God may be glorified. In verse 2, the phrase "the day of vengeance of our God" should be translated "the day of salvation of our God," because whether the Hebrew word is translated as God's just punishment of the wicked or his salvation of the needy depends entirely upon the context (see comment on 47:3).

Verse 6 suggests in a new way the mission of Israel to the world. They are to be "the priests of the Lord" and "the ministers of . . . God" (compare Exod. 19:6). As the religious teachers of all mankind they will no longer have to suffer poverty and distress.

Verses 8-9 declare God's intention to make an everlasting Covenant with Israel, one that will relate him evermore to his people (see comment on 55:3; 59:21). In the final verses of the poem the Servant is heard to reply to God's promise: he acknowledges God's salvation, declaring that what is to happen with Israel is the work of the Lord in causing "righteousness and praise to spring forth before all the nations" (vss. 10-11).

The New Jerusalem (62:1-12)

This poem repeats themes that are common in Second Isaiah in chapters 40-55 and 60-61. Zion, or Jerusalem, is the object of a prophecy in which God is represented as speaking in the first person. The closest parallel to this chapter is 51:1—52:12, where after the Servant of the Lord has responded to God's call (ch. 50), the following prophecy turns to the encouragement of Zion and foretells the city's reconstruction. Similarly, the servant poem in chapter 61 (if that is the correct interpretation) is followed again by the encouragement of Zion. Here again the subject is the New Jerusalem which is the religious capital of the world, a city no longer termed "Forsaken," but instead "*Hephzibah*" and "*Beulah*" (the Hebrew terms translated "My delight is in her" and "Married" in verse 4). She who has been forsaken, as though she were an unmarried girl, will now be married, and the occasion will be one for great rejoicing. God has placed watchmen on the walls of Jerusalem, and never again need the city be in fear (vss. 6-9). The inhabitants of the city are commanded to go out to the gates and prepare a highway on which all of the redeemed of the Lord may return (vss. 10-12). They will be called "The holy people," and the city is to be called "Sought out," a city no longer forsaken. Thus through an address to Jerusalem the current inhabitants of the very poor and as yet unfortified city are themselves encouraged and strengthened for the future which they must face, a future with meaning and significance. The Lord is the Lord of history; he is the living God; and life under his direction is an exciting prospect.

The Judgment of the Nations (63:1-6)

This brief passage has its closest parallel in chapter 34. The picture is a terrible one of a great warrior returning from bloody battle with stained garments, red as though he had been trampling the juice from grapes in a winepress (vs. 3). The prophet asks the identity of the warrior (vs. 1), and the answer comes back from God himself: "It is I, announcing vindication [victory], mighty to save." Verse 4 continues with the identification of the occasion. It is "the day of vengeance," and God's "year of redemption." The setting is the country of Edom, southeast of the Dead Sea, and one of its chief cities, Bozrah (see also 34:6). When Nebuchadnezzar's army destroyed Judah and Jerusalem in two campaigns in 597 and 587 (or 586) B.C., the people of Edom took advantage of the weakness of the Judeans and took over the whole southern part of the country, including Hebron, the natural center of the area. Thus in eschatological passages from the period of the fall of Judah and from exilic times there is repeated reference to this event, and an expression of the certainty that God in his righteousness will punish the offender. In Isaiah 63:1-6, however, the treatment is generalized, and actually the subject is the judgment of all the peoples of the world, as verses 3 and 6 seem to make clear. Verse 5 repeats the theme introduced in 59:18, where the context is the judgment of Israel.

This passage, like chapter 34, belongs with the literature of apocalyptic judgment (see especially, for example, Ezekiel 38-39; Joel 3:9-16; Zechariah 14). Behind such warlike and bloody pictures there is a profound realization of the power of evil and its influence in the world. Biblical man did not see it as possible that society could gradually evolve into God's Kingdom without a radical revolution in the human heart, and without an equally radical revolution in social and national structures within which human life is set. The mystery of this evil is indeed great; it is an evil that impels mankind to fight against its own best good—or, as Christians have interpreted the Crucifixion in the New Testament, to crucify even its Savior. The hope of man is based upon the power of God to curb this infection within all human life and its institutions. So difficult is the removal of evil from history that the Bible, in both the Old and the New Testaments, portrays the process as a warfare between God and all the forces aligned against him. In the Old Testament this warfare is against enemies on earth; in the New Testament the battle is given more cosmic dimensions in the picture of God's struggle against Satan or against the principalities and powers of darkness (for example, Ephesians 6:12 and the more figurative presentation in Revelation 12-18).

The portrayal of this future in Isaiah 63 can be called apoc-

alyptic because it is unrelated to any specified historical event.
Instead, it has to do with the final war in the age to come
against the peoples in the world who are alienated from God,
a war which must be fought and won by God before the era of
peace can be finally established. It has been frequently pointed
out that Karl Marx took this biblical picture of the necessity
of revolution, secularized it, and used it at the center of his
interpretation of history: before the classless society can be
achieved, there must be a revolution in which the capitalist
classes are destroyed. The biblical faith in the power of God to
control this virulence means that in this world mankind can
place his faith firmly only in God himself. The Marxist faith
in dialectical materialism, an overly simplified view of human
evil as belonging only to the heart and structures of bourgeois
society and not to those of the proletariat, has meant the pro-
longed dictatorship of the Communist party and the gradual
modification of the views of Marx in practice if not in theory.

A Prophetic Intercessory Prayer (63:7—64:12)

Following the terrible picture of the judgment of the nations
(vss. 1-6), there is inserted a long and beautiful intercessory
prayer on the part of the prophet. (See also the earlier intercession in 59:9-15, inserted following the description of the sin
of the newly revived postexilic community.) The date and authorship of the passage are difficult to fix. To judge from the implication of 64:10-11, Jerusalem is still a desolation and the Temple
has not been rebuilt. Thus the intercessory prayer is probably
earlier than 520 B.C. and could be of the same date as or earlier
than the prophetic poems in chapters 40-55. Whether the author
is Second Isaiah himself or another member of his school cannot be determined with certainty. The mood, the style, and the
themes all differ considerably from those that are characteristic
of Second Isaiah himself. It has been suggested that the poem is
a liturgy composed for a particular occasion. This may indeed
be the case, but it is impossible for us now to reconstruct what
that occasion was.

The intercession begins after the manner of a confessional
hymn of praise in which the worshiper recounts the glorious
deeds of God for the salvation of his people (vs. 7; see Pss.
89:1-2; 111; 145-146). The Hebrew term which is here trans-

lated "steadfast love" is one of the greatest words in the Old Testament; it refers to the unlimited grace of God which led him to visit Israel with his saving action and to create of them a people for himself and to maintain them as his people by deed and promise, in spite of their rebellion against him.

Verses 8-9 continue with a moving statement of how God had related himself to his people. He made them his people by becoming their Savior: "In all their affliction he was afflicted, and the angel of his presence saved them; in his love and in his pity he redeemed them; he lifted them up and carried them all the days of old." Unfortunately, the text of verse 9 is by no means certain. While the translation quoted is a possibility, it is equally possible that the Greek translation is correct when it takes the first words of the verse, "in all their affliction," as the completion of the previous poetic line. Also, instead of "he was afflicted" the translation has a noun meaning "messenger." The passage thus was rendered as follows: "And he became their Savior in all their afflictions. Neither ambassador nor angel but the Lord himself saved them by loving them and sparing them. He himself redeemed them and lifted them up and held them high all the days of old." The basic thought of the two different translations is the same: God has been his people's Savior and Redeemer throughout their history.

Verses 10-14 of chapter 63 are an interpretation of Israel's past history. The people rebelled, with the result that God himself had to turn against them and appear as their enemy. The subject of the sentence, "Then he remembered the days of old, of Moses his servant," is Israel. When the people were in trouble they remembered the Exodus from Egypt, the work of Moses and the power of God when Israel had been saved in a time of critical danger. The reference to God's giving his people "rest" (63:14) has rich overtones in the original language. It is not only a matter of resting from overexertion; it is also a matter of peace, quiet, and the absence of danger.

The prophet's petition now begins in 63:15 and continues through the middle of 64:5. On behalf of the people he beseeches God to remember that he is "our Father, our Redeemer from of old." That Israel, as the children of Abraham, "does not know us," "does not acknowledge us," presumably refers to the poverty in condition and numbers of the survivors of the destruction of Judah and Jerusalem as compared with the Israel of the former days. Thus the words mean that the Israel of old would not recognize the current small community as the heirs of God's promises of old.

Since all things ultimately have their origin in God, the intercessor can pray: "O LORD, why dost thou make us err from thy ways . . . ?" It is not that God is being blamed for the sins of his people. Instead, the thought is that God alone has the power to save them from themselves and their own sin. Their theocentric manner of speaking enables the biblical writers to ascribe all things to God without in the least removing the people's responsibility for their own acts. Thus Exodus 7:3 can refer to God's hardening the heart of Pharaoh whereas Exodus 8:15, 19, and 32 can refer to Pharaoh's hardening his own heart. God in his all-seeing providence and foreknowledge could employ the sin of Pharaoh for his own larger uses. So here in the prophet's intercession, while it is Israel who is responsible for her own ways, the source of the sin can be traced to God himself in the sense that he has power to use it for his own purposes and to overrule it. What appears from the standpoint of logic to be a contradiction was not apparent to biblical man nor to biblical theism generally.

In 64:1-3 there is an allusion to the disturbing events that were commonly associated with a theophany or appearance of God (see Exod. 19:16; Judges 5:5). The prophet's prayer is that God might again make himself and his power known in the earth among a people who badly need him.

The final section (from the middle of 64:5 through 64:12) constitutes the heart of the prophet's intercession. Here the speaker uses the first person plural, "we," in order to emphasize the corporate nature of the petition. We are all sinners, and yet we are also "the work of thy hand." We are all thy people, but our land is desolate. The prophet can only appeal to the mercy of God. He cannot point to any merit within his people themselves as a ground for God's saving action. But knowing that it is the nature of God to show mercy, he appeals on behalf of his people for God to show that mercy. As in all the great biblical prayers sin, understood as rebellion against God, is taken with ultimate seriousness, a seriousness with which people normally do not regard their own evil actions. The Israelite knows, however, that sin and judgment go together. There is no "cheap grace." Sin is costly, as is also redemption. The remarkable thing is that God is willing to do so much in assuming the cost of that redemption.

God's Reply to the Intercession (65:1-25)

Whether this chapter was originally composed by the author of the preceding intercessory prayer is not known. It is clear, however, that the school of Second Isaiah which put the material together in the form in which we have it, regarded the poem as God's answer to the intercession of the prophet. The evil of Israel is such that God is now going to make a division between those who are his true servants and those who will not serve him. The former will be the heirs of the new life in the new age; the latter will not. In pre-exilic prophecy the announcement of God's judgment of the people was also a call to repentance. The wedge of God's judgment was thus driven into the midst of the community, separating the true Israel from the false Israel. That separation is now drawn sharply and explicitly in this eschatological passage. The picture was to be sharpened even more in the Intertestament period when belief in the underworld to which all men went upon death was revised into a picture of hell inhabited by those whom God has judged and found past redemption.

God is the speaker in the first section of the chapter (vss. 1-7). His answer to the preceding intercession is that he was ready to be sought at all times, but Israel did not seek him. Instead, in response to his pleas, the people turned their backs and followed rebellious and idolatrous practices. Verses 8-10 give God's announcement of what he is going to do about the situation. A popular saying concerning the vineyard harvest is quoted in verse 8. Those gathering the grapes will say about a particular cluster, "Do not destroy it, for there is a blessing in it." Thus God is not going to destroy the whole people, but will save particular clusters of them who will again inhabit the Promised Land. The reference to Sharon (vs. 10) is to the northern coastal plain which in ancient times was filled with swamps. This land now will become a pasture for flocks. The Valley of Achor is probably to be identified as a barren area called today the *Buqeiah*, in the hills above Qumran where the Dead Sea Scrolls people had their monastery at the northwestern tip of the Dead Sea. This desolate place will also become a fine pasture land.

Verses 11-16 give the prophet's words to the sinners who will

not listen to God, but who indulge in worship of the pagan
deities, Gad and Meni (translated as "Fortune" and "Destiny").
Verses 13-14 quote God's decision to separate his true servants
from those who will not honor him. Then comes the explanation
that the rebels will be slain and those who remain will be purified
of all taint (vss. 15-16).

The new community having been purged, the prophet is now
free to present again the picture of the glorious age to come. It
will be a new creation, and the terror and sadness connected with
"the former things" will no longer be remembered. Jerusalem will
now be inhabited by a joyous people among whom there will be
no more weeping or distress, and no more untimely death, either
for infants or for older people. "They shall not labor in vain,
or bear children for calamity . . ." ; and God will be close to
them and will respond to their needs before they ask (vss. 23-
24). Verse 25 repeats in slightly different language the thought
of 11:6-9 including the first part of verse 9: "They shall not hurt
or destroy in all my holy mountain." The new age will see the
remedy for all that is unnatural in current history and in the life
of nature. The words in verse 25, "and dust shall be the serpent's
food," are a reference to Genesis 3:14. Presumably this means
that in the future not even snakes will be harmful; their normal
diet will be the dust of the earth.

The Coming Salvation and Judgment of God (66:1-24)

There is much about the final chapter of the Isaiah literature
which is unclear, and as a result there has been much debate
about it. For one thing, there is the problem of its fragmentary
nature. It is difficult to understand how this can be a unified
composition, because the themes shift hastily without connection
one with another. It is probable, therefore, that the disciples of
Second Isaiah have put together a number of fragments which
appear to derive from the same general period and to present the
same general point of view as chapter 65. We seem to be within
the reconstituted community of the postexilic period, perhaps
about 520 B.C. when the Temple is being rebuilt (vss. 1-2). It is
now clear to the school of Second Isaiah that God's fulfillment of
his promises of the new age with the restoration of the community in Palestine has not been as immediate or as comparatively simple as Second Isaiah himself presented it in 540 B.C.

There is to be a great salvation, but with it there is also to be a terrible judgment.

The Temple was rebuilt between 520 and 515 B.C. under the inspiration of the prophets Haggai and Zechariah (Ezra 5:1-2). Haggai told the people that all their troubles were caused by their failure to build the Temple promptly (Haggai 1:2-11). He seems to have promised the people in his day that as soon as the Temple was built, the great Day of the Lord would come (Haggai 2:2-9). This situation would appear to be the context of Isaiah 66:1-4. For the disciples of Second Isaiah, the emphasis on the importance of getting the Temple rebuilt is misplaced. God wants the inner reform which goes with the humble spirit. His primary desire is not for a Temple (see Ps. 50:7-23; Jer. 7:1-15). It is always much easier to erect a religious edifice than it is actually to be the *people* of God. Verse 3 appears to condemn sacrificial worship in the strongest possible terms. It is improbable, however, that the prophet is advocating abolition of all the outward forms of worship known at that time. He is speaking in hyperbole in order to make his point as strong as possible. What he is condemning in the name of God is an improper worship, carried on by those who have no sincerity of heart or purpose. At least, such an interpretation would be in line with that required by such comparable passages as 1:10-20; Amos 5:21-24; Micah 6:1-8. Verse 4 makes quite clear the point which the author has in mind: when God has called to the people, no one has responded; those who have elaborated their cultic worship did not choose the things in which God delights.

Verse 5 refers to a division in the community. Those being addressed by the prophet are told that God is on their side. What this division is we do not know, and it is therefore impossible to spec late about it with any certainty.

Verse 6 seems to be still another fragment. The prophet as watchman speaks of the voice of the Lord being heard in judgment, calling from the Temple, probably as a prelude to the terrible actions expected when the great Day of the Lord arrives.

Verses 7-9, in the figure of birth, portray the bringing forth of a new people. It is something that will happen very quickly, something never before heard or seen. It is possible for human mothers to be so exhausted in bringing children to the point of birth that they have no strength to bring them forth (see 37:3), but as verse 9 asserts, such a thing would not happen to God. The birth is sure.

Verses 10-14 call for general rejoicing. Jerusalem will again be in comfort and in prosperity.

Verses 15-16 could well be the sequel to verse 6. The reference is to the coming judgment of God against all his enemies. Verse 17 is a fragment that seems to specify who some of these enemies of God are felt to be: those who carry on various kinds of profane religious rites which God does not permit among his people.

Verses 18-21 revert to the frequent theme in the preceding passages about the gathering of the exiles from all over the world and their return to the "holy mountain Jerusalem." In verse 18 the thought is of all the nations streaming to Jerusalem to see the glory of the Lord. A sign will also be placed among the nations (see 49:22; 62:10). Emissaries will go to far-off Tarshish, a Phoenician metal-refining colony somewhere in the western Mediterranean (on Sardinia or in Spain), to Put and Lud in Africa, to Tubal somewhere in Asia Minor, and to Javan, the country of the Ionian Greeks in western Asia Minor.

The final verses of the chapter seem to be two different fragments. Verses 22-23 refer to the permanence and stability of the new community, and of the worship of all mankind from Sabbath to Sabbath. Verse 24, however, is perhaps one of the most repulsive verses in the whole Isaiah literature. So serious has become the prophetic disgust with one section of the new community in Jerusalem, that God's judgment upon it is taken with terrible earnestness.

The effect of that judgment is pictured as the presence of dead bodies perpetually being eaten by worms and burned with fire, without being consumed, an everlasting "abhorrence to all flesh." The author of this piece evidently felt that the situation was so terrible that this type of perpetual warning was needed.

Thus the Book of Isaiah comes to a close. The terrible suffering which would come with the fall of Jerusalem and Judah, predicted by First Isaiah, literally came to pass in 587 (or 586) B.C., but the suffering did not bring with it the removal of the proclivity to sin in the human heart. Second Isaiah (chs. 40-55) prophesied the coming salvation of Israel from exile and with it the redemption of the whole world through the Servant People who were to be purified and renewed. The final restoration of the community came to pass and the Temple was rebuilt during the latter part of the sixth century, but according to chapters 56-66 the community had not learned very much from its previous suffering. The redeemed people had not been purified of the taint of and disposition for evil. Consequently, the disciples of Second Isaiah are called upon to look forward to additional judgment and salvation in the time ahead. Judaism, beginning with the period of Ezra in the fifth century, developed the religion of the Law. While awaiting the coming of God's new age it was necessary that the whole community keep the whole body of God's revealed Law, in order that its center, the relation envisaged in the Mosaic Covenant, would not be violated. The New Testament pictures the Kingdom of God as arriving with Jesus Christ, God's Suffering Servant who in death was exalted as the Messiah (the Christ). The central issue is the problem of sin itself, the unsolved problem of Israel. The Christian doctrines of the Atonement, justification by faith, and the new life in Christ became the possession of the Church as it waited for the fulfillment in its own time of the great prophetic promises of old. Since then, Christians have learned not to expect a literal fulfillment of these promises. They are a part of inspired Scripture, however, because they proclaim faith in the God whom human sin cannot defeat. God has a purpose in his creation of the world and in his creation of the Church, the People of God. These portrayals of the future point the direction in which history must move, because God is our Lord. In this certainty, life by faith becomes a possibility, and responsible ethical decisions can be made in life now in the certainty that God will use such actions to his glory.